Leadership and School Boards

Leadership and School Boards

*Guarding the Trust in an Era of
Community Engagement
Second Edition*

Laura E. Reimer

ROWMAN & LITTLEFIELD
Lanham • Boulder • New York • London

Published by Rowman & Littlefield
A wholly owned subsidiary of The Rowman & Littlefield Publishing Group, Inc.
4501 Forbes Boulevard, Suite 200, Lanham, Maryland 20706
www.rowman.com

Unit A, Whitacre Mews, 26-34 Stannary Street, London SE11 4AB

Copyright © 2015 by Laura E. Reimer

All rights reserved. No part of this book may be reproduced in any form or by any electronic or mechanical means, including information storage and retrieval systems, without written permission from the publisher, except by a reviewer who may quote passages in a review.

British Library Cataloguing in Publication Information Available

Library of Congress Cataloging-in-Publication Data

Reimer, Laura, 1959- .
Leadership and school boards : guarding the trust in an era of community engagement / Laura E. Reimer. — Second edition.
p. cm.
Includes bibliographical references.
ISBN 978-1-4758-1506-1 (cloth : alk. paper) — ISBN 978-1-4758-1507-8 (pbk. : alk. paper) — ISBN 978-1-4758-1508-5 (electronic)
1. School boards—North America. 2. Educational leadership—North America. 3. Democracy. I. Title.
LB2831.R45 2015
379.1'531097—dc23
2015019514

∞ ™ The paper used in this publication meets the minimum requirements of American National Standard for Information Sciences Permanence of Paper for Printed Library Materials, ANSI/NISO Z39.48-1992.

Printed in the United States of America

For my dad, Edgar Burleigh Wilson.

You have been the wind beneath my wings, all the days of my life. It was your belief in me and your tireless and successful campaign management that catapulted me into the world of school board governance.

And for my sister Margo Wilson Kehler, a master teacher whose passion for excellence and belief in the value of education has never wavered, and whose school board has steadily equipped such vision.

Contents

Foreword		ix
Preface to the Second Edition		xiii
How to Use This Book		xvii
1	Local Democracy: Overview of the School Board Contribution	1
2	Complex Arena of Democracy: Influences on the School Board	15
3	Community Democracy: The Power of Engagement	27
4	Governing Democracy: The Politics of Education	41
5	Democratic Leadership: Board Chair as First Among Equals	55
6	Active Democracy: The Collective Strength of School Board Members	71
7	Ensuring Democracy: The Answerability of School Boards	87
8	Encouraging Democracy: Carefully Designed Culture	105
9	Modeling Democracy: Leadership in Action	117
10	Administering Democracy: The Superintendent and CEO	127
Conclusion: Leading Democracy: The Governing School Board		137
Bibliography		145
About the Author		149

Foreword

Every day children all over North America leave their homes to attend schools within the communities where they live. It's something they and we, their parents, grandparents and neighbors all take for granted. Very few of us take time to think about who ensures that there will be good schools to go to, that they will be warm and safe, that they will be run by qualified teachers and other caring adults, that they will help our children and young people to find their place and make their way in the world. Very few of us really understand that schools are the result of our belief in the goodness of democracy and, in fact, are an essential underpinning of our democratic society. And many don't know that democracy, our way of life, is created and recreated first in schools and in the people we elect to govern them, our school trustees and the school boards who represent the democratic ideal in action.

Laura E. Reimer, in this guide to school governance called, *Leadership and School Boards: Guarding the Trust in an Era of Community Engagement*, reminds us and revitalizes our understanding of the crucial role that local school boards play in the building and rebuilding of our democratic foundations. Laura is a passionate advocate of school boards but she has not allowed her advocacy to cloud the high standards she sets for them and the high expectations she has of them. At the same time as she reminds us that we owe a huge debt of gratitude to the selfless commitment of most of our public school trustees, she reminds all trustees that on their shoulders rest the hopes of our nations that our young will understand, uphold and enjoy the human benefits of living in great democracies. On the one hand, it's a tough act to get right; on the other, it is a most joyful public trust and responsibility—there is no higher calling!

In an easy-to-read coherent and comprehensive way, Laura takes us through the familiar but ever new, political-ethical road map of educational politics and community engagement, educational leadership and collective responsibility, educational governance and school community culture intertwining the conceptual and the practical seamlessly. She provides us insights into the importance of moral disagreement and compromise, democratic contestation amid an invitation to political dialogue by and for all, and education as the great preparation for living your life well among others who are also trying to live their lives well, often in different ways but always in the interest of the good of all. Throughout her major focus remains the same—trustees are essential to the functioning of schools and society and they collectively have a moral responsibility to all citizens both within and beyond the local community—trustees make education possible.

To make education possible, Laura expects them to be leaders, act like leaders and to choose good leaders. While she is willing to grant trustees the personal recognition she believes they deserve, she emphasizes that they are a body corporate and that there is no room and must be no tolerance for self-serving and self-aggrandizing rogue trustees. As in all corporate bodies one person, the chair, is chosen from their own ranks to be a leader for a time and she lays out very succinctly but comprehensively what the board should be able to expect from that office – firmness, fairness, decorum and civility and a commitment to education and the people charged with ensuring that our children and young people get the best we can offer in terms of schooling.

She then proceeds to explain how that leadership, in turn, results in strong, responsive and accountable (I like her introduction of the term "answerability") representation to and for the community, and assists other parts of the community in building and living the healthy community ideal.

Near the end, unequivocally and unblinkingly, Laura addresses what has turned out to be perhaps the most contentious and conflict-ridden aspect of trusteeship, that being choosing, working with and supporting the Superintendent and CEO. She draws a clean distinction between governance as responsibility of the board and administration a responsibility of the Superintendent and CEO. She, a former board member and I, a longtime superintendent and CEO, agree on the division of authority and responsibility as she lays it out. But it is not all conflict and contention between the roles as she lays them out. We also agree that, when the two offices are defined by deep knowledge, mutuality, reciprocity and respect, there is no better relationship anywhere in politics and education.

Laura E. Reimer is now, as she has always been, a caring teacher, a thinking learning and an insightful scholar of life and living. Her experience as a trustee was not wasted on her and this book is a reflection of who she is and what she believes—and she believes in the goodness of her fellow human beings. Her aims, her positions, her organization, her real world examples and her pauses for reflection resonate deeply with someone like me who has been an educator for five decades and an educational administrator for over thirty-five of those years, and has attended well over a thousand board meetings. This book is meant for everybody interested in what goes on in the school system—trustees, superintendents and other administrators, teachers, parents, community members, students in colleges and universities. Reading it will reveal the powerful and practical insights of a person who has made the pursuit of

democracy, education and the improvement of the human condition a lifelong pursuit.
John R. Wiens, PhD
Dean Emeritus and Professor of Education
The University of Manitoba

Preface to the Second Edition

School boards shape society through systems of education. They choose who leads the systems and how educators are selected to lead classrooms. They approve the allocation of millions of dollars every year. As leaders, school board members determine how their community defines the values, resources, and belief systems that together form the democratic mosaic of our times. Imbedded within this knowledge are timeless foundations that have carried us from the origins of school boards to our current systems; these are the keys to community engagement, and these are the keys to empowered and strong school systems.

This book is about the remarkable and unique purpose of school boards. It is not a book about abolition or drastic reform. It explains clearly that school boards were established as part of the foundation for a strong democratic society and encourages everyone involved with school systems to guard that foundation. School boards embody the most immediate principles of democracy. This is an exciting book, appropriate for our times, focused on the powerful leadership necessary in the school board, and the potential to deliver ever-improving results through consistent and deliberate governance.

School boards are comprised of elected and appointed members. In the United States and in Canada, virtually all school systems, public and private, faith-based and secular, are governed by school boards. The role, the contributions, and especially the influence of school boards are among modern democracy's hidden treasures—not because they are mysterious, but because so few people have opportunities to learn about school boards.

With few exceptions we do not teach students from kindergarten through university about the remarkable governance plan that ultimately and democratically reflects community through the work of school boards. Without a great plan, and certainly without a working knowledge of such a plan, problems remain inadequately addressed, policies do not achieve their goals, and well-intended programs become mostly expensive.

Governing and overseeing the administration of learning is a unique competency that sets school boards apart. This book combines many experiences, books, and articles with principles of meaningful community engagement to explain the original purpose of school boards, and how that plan relevantly informs school board excellence today.

Despite significant criticism and reform, school boards have continued to endure. In the years since the first edition of this book was published, many new internal and external issues have confronted school board members. Funding, organizational expansion and change, bullying, teacher evaluation, gang involvement, newcomers from war-torn states, changing demographics, and social media are some of the issues that threaten to deter school boards from their central focus of governance.

Good governance is, by its very structure and intent, an excellent plan for strong and relevant leadership, regardless of the issues. In the end, no matter how distressing or conflictual the issues may be, the intended role of the school board to acknowledge, address, and respond to these issues as strong governors of the district remains remarkably unchanged. Through consistent patterns of governance, school boards can deliver better and better results despite the lure of micromanagement invited by the issues of the day. When school boards govern steadily, our communities are strengthened as a result of their work.

While school boards face difficult and potentially divisive issues—matters that threaten the foundations of our communities—the best responses are found in the strengths of school boards. After careful contemplation of much literature and of school board websites, it is apparent that the answer to all of these remains most profoundly situated in good school board governance. Good governance is the constant and steady leadership required in our rapidly changing world, and it is designed to lead our school systems!

While it is tempting for board members to deflect and avoid conflict, the real work of the school board member is to empower the assets and resources within the people, organizations, and institutions that share the local school district. Such relationships and empowerment will inevitably lead to appropriate responses and solutions, directly reflect local values and belief systems, and lend strength and guidance to the community at large.

In other words, the best and most appropriate responses to local, regional, national, and global issues at the local level are still found by school boards that truly represent their communities. Consequently, community engagement and the tremendous potential for much needed leadership by school boards is a theme that threads throughout this book. The closest democratic representation of community is the school board.

Recent literature offers assistance to the work of school boards; few pinpoint the unique governance of school boards. Rowman & Littlefield Education publications are available online and include outstanding references about the ongoing work of school boards. Readers are specifically encouraged to consult Thomas L. Alsbury's *The Future of School Board Governance: Relevancy and Revelation* published in 2008, and Doug Eadie's seminal work *Five Habits of High-Impact School Boards* for expanded information

Books such as these are important because school boards are unique. General board governance literature is not completely relevant for effective school board governance. School boards are different from general boards of directors in many ways, but primarily because their corporate product is learning. There is a combined strength of partnership at the school board table between locally elected representation (the trustees or board members) and education administrative expertise (the CEO/superintendent).

This book was originally published in 2008 as *Leadership and School Boards: Guarding the Trust*. We live in an important time, wherein democracy is often misunderstood and is certainly under attack. The first edition has been enhanced in this second book, in which the central message is engagement. School boards still contain the keys to strong democratic states.

Within this message of community engagement are knowledge, support, and clarity of purpose to all those individuals who are involved in some way with the work of school boards—from interested citizens to elected members of government, from students of public policy and education to the policy advisors in all levels of government.

The book you are reading challenges individuals to understand the purpose and responsibilities of school boards and board members. It is intended to equip citizens to choose their school boards wisely, and to perhaps seek office themselves. The book enlightens people working within and outside the school system to the tremendous potential for fulfilled opportunities within the board room when the board decides to lead, engage, and govern purposefully.

There have been some important additions to the book, and updates have been made throughout. Notably, there is a new chapter about community engagement, which is an emerging area of scholarship but not a new responsibility for school boards. The second edition demonstrates how the principles of good school board governance remain the most appropriate and effective way to respond to the many new and difficult issues confronting school boards today. Also, the chapter about the role of the board chair offers some effective skills and techniques for recognizing and managing conflict.

Finally, this book is intended to encourage school board members to embrace contagious and enthusiastic leadership. Visions are powerful, and our school systems need boards of strong and tireless vision, fueled by the strength of excellent administration, and the hopes, dreams, and resources of the local community.

The usual critics of school boards may never be silenced, but when individual board members pick up the challenge, recognize how critical it is that they fulfill their unique roles at the helm of the school district, and take action, the rest of us will see the school systems we want for our children. Consistently good governance means that critics of school boards will be forced to acknowledge that the local school board leads society with engaged and relevant democracy.

This book and its predecessor are the products of my own experiences at two school board tables, service for education at the state and national levels, my personal training, research, and formal education, and consultation work I did with school boards in urban, rural, and Native communities. It also evolved over cups of coffee with people I respect greatly, and experiences with people who were less endearing but were certainly motivating. I often miss my time at an effective school board table, but not my time at a table that has lost its way.

Although I have had assistance with the concept, writing, and editing of the book, any mistakes or shortcomings are entirely mine.

School boards are imperative to our democracy and can provide tremendous models for other levels of government. Most importantly, they can readily engage and empower their communities to ensure a meaningful tomorrow. It is my hope that courageous school board leadership in this era of community democracy will be characterized by courage, tenacity, and creativity, so that all across society we will reap the benefits of great school board governance.

—Laura E. Reimer, PhD
Winnipeg, Manitoba, Canada
2015

How to Use This Book

This is a guide to the vibrant leadership school board members can bring to the communities they represent and the school systems they govern. The book provides the original and still relevant plan for school boards, set forth in early legislation, describes the independent yet interactive roles of those who serve at the board table, and discusses how community engagement, as part of strong governance practices, continues to be the critical and unique contribution school boards can bring to western democracy.

This book is for the school board and its community, which makes up the diverse audience that is deeply invested in excellent school board governance. This book is for those within the educational community. This includes long-serving, and new board members, parents, guardians, and parent council members, teachers, student teachers, university students, professors, and those who study, teach, and facilitate effective governance and administration. However, the book is also for members of the general public who may aspire one day to serve at the school board table, and it is for every voter who elects our school board members.

The second edition expands the first edition with the continued goal of developing strong, effective, community-engaged school boards. Each chapter within this second edition has been rewritten and updated to address the issues and practices unique to school board governance. Although governance does not change, school boards serve in an ever-changing environment, to which the second edition of this book adapts.

At the end of each chapter are questions and applications. These are intended to provoke both thought and discussion in the context of local realities, so that readers may apply the core concepts of each chapter in meaningful and practical ways to their own school boards. Readers are encouraged to understand the original democratic purpose of school boards in practical terms, and are provided with some examples of school board actions that fail to reflect good governance and the plan for democratic community engagement and representation.

The questions are also intended to engage readers so that the principles outlined in this book can be applied. They are intended to guide discussion, provide potential essay topics for college and university students, or prompt critical consideration by serving board members. For post-secondary institutions, or for innovative educators wishing to expand the knowledge of their students regarding the role of the school board that governs their own district, this book may be used as a textbook, as each chapter corresponds with one week in an academic term.

This book fills a niche among school board books. It is not a criticism, a call for abolition, or a call for reform. Rather, this book simply contains tools to connect the dreams of the people in our neighborhoods to the practices at the school board table. In one volume, *Leadership and School Boards: Guarding the Trust in an Era of Community Engagement, Second Edition* highlights and explains the incredibly meaningful contributions inherent in our modern school boards, which, when incorporated into governance practices by school board members across the nation, will assure the fulfillment of local visions and a great tomorrow for today's students, community members, and educators.

ONE

Local Democracy

Overview of the School Board Contribution

Our local communities, and the schools within them, are the very heart of democracy. Within these communities lie the assets, the hopes and dreams, the resources, and the people who shape the world around us. Democracy, most simply defined, is the right to choose one's leadership. Participating in the selection of leaders and in the development of tomorrow's leaders is a vibrant tenet of democracy. School boards have a critical role in the growth and continuance of our democratic society. Democracy is fragile, and without great governance, especially at the school board level, it is threatened.

Democracy is a governing system that brings many minds together so that bigger dreams may be achieved for individuals, for communities, for the nation, and for society at large. This is achieved, in part, through the establishment and maintenance of excellent school system governance. As a member of the school board, the potential to impact lives for continuous learning and improvement is unparalleled in public service and in community work. As a board, seven to nine elected people join with highly trained educational experts to meet several times a month to chart the future of our schools, which in turn, charts the future of our democracy.

With this great potential, how is it that not all school boards are excellent examples of good governance? Why do board members debate whether or not students should be allowed to wear hats in school, instead of leveraging the potential for asset-based partnerships in their communities to achieve that which may seem impossible for their schools? In fact, school boards can be motivational leaders to establish the school systems we know we want. Although many are not trained to govern well, learning to govern with excellence is not difficult, but does require courage and tenacity.

Despite drastic changes in the structures and administration of education, the potential for school boards to engage community and influence student learning in a continuously positive manner remains steadfast. Prosperity and poverty, increased public scrutiny, escalating public expectations, time pressure, global issues, cultural integration, diminishing resources, and relentless attacks from other levels of government are just some of the external challenges facing our school boards.

Regardless, school board members can lead with courage and vision when they understand the pivotal and unique role of school board governance and determine to do the critical and empowering job to which they were elected. Many school boards lack focus; excellent school boards focus on the processes of governance to produce results.

With a singular goal of good governance, school board members can navigate the most difficult waters and unanticipated issues by maintaining their focus on the task that only they can perform—ensuring that the district is well run and representative of local priorities, values, and cultures. Great school boards lead with careful attention to wise and consistent leadership, which is protected through vigilant attention to good board policy.

Although there are some fine examples of school boards that offer compelling leadership and vision, too many board members are elected to office without a clear understanding of what they are supposed to do. The sincerity of those citizens, willing to devote years to serving their local school district as elected board members, is not in doubt, but the confusion of board members regarding their role has augmented the ineffectiveness of school boards in a number of areas. Board members who want to provide administrative or professional functions must step back from the governance table. They are elected only to govern.

Although it is almost impossible to measure motivation or intent, it is apparent that most elected members of the school board do the best they can with whatever form of governance has evolved in their jurisdictions. Folks are elected, and usually reelected, by well-intended voters who also do not know what they ought to expect from their school board members. This grave problem frustrates everyone who needs skilled school board governors, and is one of the substantive reasons for this book.

This book presents the strength, purpose, and compelling role of school board leadership, which has always been part of school boards. It discusses the historical and democratic purposes of school boards, expands on the concept of democratic engagement inherent within the role of the school board, and explains the practical leadership tasks and actions of good governance. Then, the roles and relationships of the board chair, board members, and superintendent are carefully presented, so that the vibrant model of democratic school board governance can be well understood and practiced. For those external to the school system, including school board members of the future, the book provides an equipping and empowering education!

THE MODERN SCHOOL BOARD

Achieving vision is about engaging community, and it is this strength that can set school boards apart in significant ways from other levels of elected officials. Good governance is about vision, oversight, and deliberate practice—not about mastery of the complicated nuances of the education industry, or about debating matters that should have been decided by district administrators and have little effect on continuous improvement at the board level.

School board members are elected to engage with their communities so as to not only create an environment to assure the achievement of district goals, but also to carefully and mindfully evaluate and assess those goals. Mediocrity can and must be pushed away from school boards. No one gets elected to fail. All school board members can fulfill the noble democratic goals for which the boards were originally established, and voters can demand the best from the community members they elect to represent them.

Excellent school board governance takes fortitude, commitment, and a resolve to think relentlessly beyond what is happening now and toward a better future. Why, then, does the electorate—and even senior government—allow tepid or destructive school board members to continue in office, usually for many years? The answer is simple: The voters do not know that board members are underperforming, or that they can effect change.

There are reasons for this lack of understanding. For example, the parents of school-age children often understand the consequences of underperforming school boards, but they comprise less than a third of all eligible voters (most voter demographics are retired seniors). Educators are also aware when they have a problematic school board, but their professionalism prevents them from telling parents and the public what is happening in the schools and classrooms in ways that correlate such matters with the ballot box.

Finally, the elected members themselves add to the lack of general understanding: The members of underperforming boards tend to keep a very low public profile and use the solidarity of governance principles as the excuse. Modern governance is perceived to be difficult because some board members themselves have complicated and confused it. Board members forget that the sincere respect of their community is more a governance role than demanding more money from the state. They forget that valuing and respecting school-community relationships is more important than arguing about what time the school bells ring.

Meanwhile, despite their legislative and other interferences, senior governments seem reluctant to abandon the institution of school boards completely. Although the amalgamation of districts has become increasingly common, and there is a constant chatter about reform and abolition, there is a recognition that as America's ground-level, democratically elected institutions, school boards are worth retaining.

It is only a lack of will that prevents us from having excellent and extraordinary school boards. Somewhere along the way, many school board members have lost their confidence to lead. They are not sure how to engage their communities, and voters do not recognize the critical need for analysis of the performance of their school board members as representatives of community values, resources, and belief systems before casting their votes.

But political structure is on the side of school boards. School boards provide the oversight, foresight, and monitoring function for school districts, and they are uniquely structured to combine local assets and resources to build stronger and more self-reliant district communities. When board members engage the public to determine a common vision, communicate value for money to their citizenry, understand what they are elected to do, and then do it, criticisms of school boards will dissipate.

There are excellent and sincere school board members serving our communities, and there are some entire school boards that understand and execute outstanding governance leadership. Many board members, though, are elected to board tables with no vision or passion for improved schools, and succumb readily to hierarchical, bureaucratic notions of power and authority. According to studies, many school board members, assume the school board office for selfish reasons that include new friendships and status, an extra paycheck, a diversion from their personal lives, or enough name recognition, seek to acquire a higher elected office.

It is time that those school board members who sit at the board table for the wrong reasons be compelled to give more and to engage more with those they represent, or be motivated to step down as soon as possible. We can no longer afford the apathy or lack of governance skill that has gripped some of America's school boards.

INTEGRAL TO LOCAL GOVERNANCE

Keys to a great society have been handed to the school boards. School board members often think that they have to look for solutions to problems: In fact, they just have to choose the best recommendations for their communities, which are often provided by community members and crafted into board decisions by the experts in the district employ.

On its website, America's National School Boards Association describes the work of school boards this way:

> As an integral part of the American institution of representative governance, local school boards have a crucial role to play in preserving our democracy, preparing our children to be productive citizens, and enriching the lives of our communities . . .
>
> In a time of social, economic, technological and geopolitical turbulence, the local school board remains the tried and true governance mechanism for delivering excellence and equity in public education for all of our children.

This role has not changed.

For the sake of our future, the future of our children, and the ongoing efforts of our professional educators, local school boards must catch and embrace the many possibilities of improving the processes of education through a focus on the excellent processes of good governance and authentic community engagement. Democracy needs good school board members. America, and the world beyond its borders, is ready for the fruit of strong, relevant local governance and the democratic freedoms that strong school boards can provide.

Whichever corner of the country we live in, we know we want amazing schools and outstanding school systems. Our school board members are elected to provide them, and we expect that our school boards are ensuring an excellent school experience for our students and educators. We elect people to the school board to take care of things for us and make sure that the schools are well run and well equipped. Ultimately, we want the next generation to stand on our shoulders. We expect that our schools will partner with us to nurture children toward adulthood and the full potential of their learning abilities.

THE POWER OF SHARED VISION

A group of people sharing the same vision is powerful. From such vision, or plan for the future, come policies and programs that often preoccupy time at the school board table. Our country stands as a mighty and inspirational example of the power of visionary leadership. Just as our forefathers forged a great country, so good school boards must embrace challenges that could easily discourage less dedicated leaders, and press on to fulfill the goal of excellent education. Board members must refuse to stand down against the adversaries of good governance, and together promote continuous improvement.

On the school board, the members can be inspiring leaders, elected with confidence and pleasure by an informed and discerning populace.

Such members recognize that the relationship between the community and the school board is a synergistic partnership that draws on strengths, assets, resources, and vision. We envision extraordinary school systems being so commonplace that their excellence is ordinary.

The role of the school board is intended to be a pivotal one. Modern students have more funding, infrastructure, personnel, and teacher expertise ready to serve their learning needs than at any other time in the history of western civilization. Despite the hard work and stated intentions of the school board members, many school boards have generally drifted into a state of obscurity and irrelevance, and this is evidenced by the constant reform to which they are subjected by other levels of government.

This can change. With an understanding of their roots and purpose, a clear vision or plan for the future, and systematic and purposeful engagement with their communities, school boards can be powerful governors that can chart a bold destiny for tomorrow's generations. In this way, school boards can inspire good governance in other governments, while seeing the fruit of their efforts in the caliber of people graduating from their schools.

School boards have the responsibility and the authority to ensure gains and high of success throughout each school system. To do so, they must govern an organization with a culture in which people are encouraged to learn, to teach, and to grow. The board has the responsibility to provide the resources required for educators to forge desired results. This takes a lot of work, thought, and purposeful interaction with the communities involved, and such real work cannot be mistakenly assumed by politically appealing campaign slogans.

Boards have interested communities, sophisticated administrations, and highly trained educators ready to make dreams realities for students. Greatness is measured by track records, not motivations or intentions, and school boards and their members have many opportunities to evidence greatness.

JUDGE THE TRACK RECORD

Contrary to intent, most school board track records do not reflect great leadership, and it is important that interested parties read the public minutes to understand whether school board members are upholding the main focus of the district, and whether they are making meaningful decisions. Many school board members have not learned to avoid the enticements of administrative meddling and busyness, and others hide behind meaningless board minutes.

As leaders they have failed to articulate an engrossing vision and may have failed to adequately provide the resources that assure a maximized learning experience for each learner every day. A quick review of the school board minutes on any website demonstrates quickly whether or not a board has actually made decisions, and if those decisions reflect democratic engagement and great leadership. While no school board member intentionally undermines professional educators and the important work of schools, current literature suggests that school boards do more to hinder than to help, and tend to be reactive rather than proactive governors.

Although there are great school boards, there is a common understanding that most school boards are ineffective and irrelevant, responsive to deficits and cutbacks rather than to pursuing their vision. They become problem-focused rather than engaged in capacity development. Many books have been written criticizing the lack of capacity and weak board development common at the modern school board table, but focusing on deficiencies and errors has never brought sustained, positive results.

To accomplish the work of schools, board members must deliberately choose to be strong and bold governors. Such a purpose gives energy! But this also involves active engagement, time, knowledge, and, at times, the heart of a lion. A lack of focus and purpose is reflected in weak or scarce track records. The results are only as strong as the source, and when it is good governance, it is sustainable. A review of the origins and original purposes of school boards empowers one to understand why local strong governance is vital, especially in education.

THE ORIGINAL SCHOOL BOARDS

Understanding the original purpose of school boards is very important because that purpose has not changed since their creation during the early decades of the country. Local school boards protect many of North America's cherished political and cultural values, and as we continue to become increasingly multicultural, the importance of strong school board governance increases.

School boards protect everyone, and education is important to this protection. Democracy requires an educated electorate in order to fulfill its mandate, and in this way, learning institutions and democracy are intertwined. The purposes of public education and of democracy run parallel through their histories, and meet at the school board table. The mandate of school boards to be excellent governors cannot be more important.

School board members carry a responsibility that has been shared throughout democratic history: to press toward a vision of society that is bigger than what we now are. Our forefathers led the population forward, and recognized that through locally relevant schools, the country could grasp a future in which our nation would be the envy of the world.

When writing about the education of the public, Thomas Jefferson was convinced that when people are well informed, they could be trusted with their own government. This is the core of democracy: the right to choose one's leadership in all contexts. Most immediately, well-informed people can choose the school board members who will best ensure that dreams for the learning potential within schools become realities.

Jefferson declared that local school governance would press the values of the community into the schools of America, develop and nurture students toward adulthood and, within a generation, strengthen the entire country. As stated, this mantle falls to the district school board. Responsibility is borne by each elected school board member when citizens vote to determine who will serve on their behalf.

Board members must be mindful that they either protect or weaken democracy and education with each decision they make at the board table. According to these tenets of democracy, school board members who fail to respect the community's values regarding schools and the school system, and who continuously outrage their communities, should not be returned to office. But typically they are. School board members are intended to represent the values of the community, not to impose their personal views on the schools, or worse, to use the office for personal gain.

THE EARLIEST DEMOCRATIC STATES

The historical roots of school boards reflect their critical leadership role in the development of our modern society. During colonial times, America was governed by a sovereign who had little knowledge, understanding, or apparent interest in North American experiences and conditions. This resulted in a general public distrust of distant government, and the perceived irrelevance of macropolitical experts in the context of local matters. Eventually, this distrust led to independence from British rule.

The widely held convictions regarding the inappropriateness of distant government affected the foundational decisions that govern education. As a result, the developing United States (and later, Canada) established elected school boards of three to five laymen. The boards were purposed to be occupied by people (men, at the time) who were familiar to citizens and who could make decisions in consideration of local values, goals, challenges, and resources.

Initially, each school was situated in a central location in the district, and board members were entrusted to provide community oversight and direct governance insight to the activities of that one school. The central purpose of school board members was to press local values into the schools of their jurisdictions. Teachers who did not uphold or respect the values of the particular new colony in which they served were replaced by the school board. The schools were to reflect the values, hopes, and dreams of the community, which were guarded by elected school boards.

Early board members recognized the responsibility they bore as representatives of all members of their community in the decisions and directions of the school. Mindful of the larger democracy taking shape in America, the school boards realized that choices made in the schools would influence the children, and so the future. They established the critical influence of local school board leadership through governance and offered general rules and direction, while the schoolteachers exercised operational authority and oversaw the teaching of reading, writing, and calculating skills.

The core work intended for school boards has remained virtually unchanged in the decades—even centuries—since their establishment in the late 1700s. The early school board members sought to establish and guard integrity, honor, values, and justice in the operations of the school. Their key contributions were not the skills they had acquired as pioneers or their knowledge of education, but rather their ability to uphold the sacred trust of their constituency in matters of character.

The reputation of the school board, rather than the professional or technical training of its membership, enabled the school boards to implement policy and provide leadership through difficult times. This community trust remains the critically required contribution of each school board member, but the one that has perhaps eroded the most in the reputation of the modern school board.

There were, and are still, very few restrictions on who can run for election for the duties performed by a school board member. The ability of successful candidates to reflect the educational aspirations of local voters is evaluated through the ballot processes at the end of each term of office; this process reflects a commitment to both democracy and accountability. School board members form a critical link between senior levels of government and the role of the school in the community in which they live and work. The school board is the public's most immediate form of democracy and protector of liberties.

THE 1900S

By the 1900s, the responsibilities of school boards expanded beyond one school, and most school boards had increased to include seven to nine board members. These lay people were responsible for developing local education policy within the parameters laid down in legislation and regulation, yet had to be ever mindful that they were at the board table as community representatives. As education grew in importance, the

American federal government continued to play a significant role in education.

Toward the end of the twentieth century, when confidence in school boards declined to its lowest, the United States established a federal department responsible for education. In Canada, education of the general public is a provincial responsibility, and so federal activity takes place mostly through government agencies and departments for indigenous (aboriginal) people. Across North America, where they express their views, federal governments are encouraging school boards to follow their mandates and govern well.

Regardless of the involvements of other levels of government, and no matter how many members sit at the board table, the school board members serve as representatives of the community. School board members liaise between the school district and the community. They are not, and must not try to serve as, educational experts. School board members are elected to be governance experts, with a tight focus on education governance.

THE BIRTH OF THE LARGE SCHOOL DISTRICT

Despite the noble intentions of democratic local representation, history tells us that many late twentieth-century city school boards reflected the distant governorship and irrelevant policy we dispensed with at great cost in 1774! The turpitude in the city boards led to cries for school board reform, and school districts were collapsed so that they could be more easily monitored. These reforms attempted to reduce corruption and to maintain the separation between education governance and general-purpose government.

The intention of reform was ultimately the protection of democracy and the priority of maximized educational capacity. The modern school district was established as a large central board for each district, with a professional chief executive with the title of superintendent placed in charge, responsible for leading the daily operations and outcomes of the district. These protections are still represented in the large school districts of today, and are part of the trust guarded by the school boards.

Each district established its own administration responsible to the superintendent and not the board. The superintendent, however, was in turn accountable to the board for the operation or management of the entire district. The intent behind centralized administrations was better education for students. School boards were still intended to reflect local values. The central role of the superintendent, now often also a chief executive officer, makes it happen. The board members, through their relationships with the community, monitor these happenings against the goals of the district with policy and with an annual superintendent evaluation.

The increased geography and demographics of larger districts seemed to confuse board members and it was not, in fairness, entirely their fault. As board members became increasingly removed from the communities that elected them, some felt powerless and so neglected strong local governance in favor of meddling in specific classroom matters. Others abdicated governance to the district administration and began to engage in other nonproductive behaviors, many of which included improper involvement in daily school matters.

However, the democratic legitimacy of school boards allows for the electorate only, and no one else, to curb these actions (as the chief employee of the board, the superintendent can only suggest and hope for behavioral changes among board members). As they became increasingly disenfranchised with their school boards, and school board members lost their visions for the district as an extension of the community, local voters lost their interest and abstained from voting. Large districts with debilitated and ineffective governing boards became the norm.

MICROMANAGEMENT

Without the governance oversight intended for the school board, school districts began to experience the crippling effects of micromanagement and purposeless vision. As a consequence in this change of governance behaviors, the school boards and their communities continued to disconnect and the credibility of the school board crumbled. Although school board members were elected to represent their communities, most were unable to maintain productive relationships with their communities or to translate community values to district policies and practices.

As school board members relinquished their leadership roles, continued befuddlement about the purpose of the school board resulted in misunderstandings and confused leadership in both the community and at the board table. As districts expanded, citizens lost sight of their ability to influence education policy, and their relationships with their local representatives seemed to evaporate. Citizens who had not experienced effective school boards ran for office and carried this leadership void to the elected table as board members. As all of these factors converged, many school boards lost their grip on educational governance.

Well-intended but uninformed board members began to involve themselves more and more in the daily work of the school district, which overlapped with the responsibilities of hired education professionals and caused interference, frustration, and difficulty that is still in evidence in many school districts today.

Perhaps most grave was the fact that this behavioral norm left the governance role empty, and superintendents were placed in the unenviable position of trying to lead and guide the board while reporting to it. When school board members ignore their legal and moral responsibilities, or assume that their personal interpretation of these responsibilities will suffice, school districts are left to deliver education without the functional leadership of the elected board.

CONSEQUENCES OF THE FAILURE TO LEAD AND GOVERN

School boards now sustain frequent attacks and criticisms from many walks of society—including other governing bodies and politicians—primarily because of the long and now habitual tendency to abandon their leadership role and to neglect their important perspective as the community voice. This is a grave matter for school systems and for society because no one else in the organization is authorized to fill the critical role of governance.

When the board fails to lead and the governance function is ignored by board members, morale and motivation wane inside the district while allegations of irrelevance, wasteful spending, and public demands for abolishment of school boards increase outside the school district. The board then spends its energy arguing with its constituency and further alienating it, instead of serving and leading on its behalf. This is distressing to most educational professionals, who recognize the vital connection between democracy, school board leadership, and highly successful schools.

Abdicated leadership has far-reaching effects for school boards beyond the district. The weakened board function prompts criticism and confrontation from parents, citizens, politicians, and even employees. The apathy of school board member voter turnout is an indication of just how irrelevant some school board members have become to the constituency they represent.

Citizens must mindfully exercise their democratic responsibilities when electing school board members, rather than just their right to vote (or to abstain), for the sake of all of our futures. Obfuscation is continued when voters select school board candidates carelessly and reelect board members who have abdicated their fiduciary and community responsibilities. Voters must recognize how critical it is to elect qualified people who will assure steadfast and relevant governance leadership for school systems.

SUMMARY

This chapter has introduced the philosophical purpose of school boards and the strengths and intentions of good governance. A brief summary of Thomas Jefferson's vision for school boards, and the historical evolution of school boards in America, created the context for the state of today's school boards. Most importantly, the chapter outlines the foundations for the critical roles for school boards in modern democracy. In large part, this role is to access and leverage local values and beliefs, and to maintain strong relationships with the stakeholders in the school system.

Our educational systems have developed in such a way that those school boards that fail to do these things are not penalized, though children pay the price. However, it would be best for all of society if school boards would encourage the adaptation of the district's organizational structure to feed and sustain learning. This fosters a strong and continued democratic society.

The school board was established to ensure that schools exist for the common good, and to uphold local values through elected guardianship of the public school system. Each school board member is responsible for representing all members of his/her constituency, and to influence decisions with their interests in mind. The school board is a critical liaison between the school system and the public.

As lawmakers, decision-makers, and bodies of appeal, school boards embody and uphold the basic elements of American democracy. They can do this with exciting and relevant leadership, mindful of their important role in the continuance of democracy, and in an environment of increasing and distracting influences still provide functional and inspiring leadership through strong governance.

QUESTIONS

1. What local values and beliefs are central in your community? Are these reflected by the initiatives and voting patterns of your school board members.
2. Take stock of the intended governance role of school boards. How has this informed your choices for school board elections in your community? What evidence will you use to evaluate the current board members?
3. Think about the school board in your district. According to its conduct and interactions with your community (and not considering formal statements of purpose or vision), what would you identify as its central purpose? List five things you know about the school board, the district, and how these inform you about the effectiveness of your school board?

APPLICATION

Go to the website of your school district and locate the public minutes. Go through one official year of minutes, logging what decisions the board made. What do these findings tell you about the school board? What is the central strength of this school board? Are there opportunities for the school board to improve its governance role?

TWO

Complex Arena of Democracy

Influences on the School Board

Governance is the integral leadership role that only the school board can provide, and the central purpose for the existence of the school board in modern America. Most boards do not recognize that governance can and must remain steadfast within an increasingly complex arena. The board's mandate is to oversee the activities of the district, but there are many influences affecting the work of the board. Few people in the general citizenry understand this. In reality, school boards still struggle with their mandate because people who are confused about the school board's role are elected, and the multiple other influences on school board governance offer compelling distractions.

Over recent decades, in both Canada and the United States, there have been renewed calls for reform. While critics may recognize the responsibilities of the school boards, they do not understand if the school board is achieving its purposes through its publicly funded existence, and instead pull the board toward nongovernance goals through whatever influence they may have.

The good news is that criticisms are targeted at the decisions within the mandate of the board. This means that public dissatisfaction with education is the primary responsibility of those sitting at the school board tables. It is the role of the board to help the constituency understand why the district is the way it is, and where there are concerns, to find solutions that everyone can live with. In this way, the influences of distraction and criticism can become strengths.

The reputation of the board is another significant influence. A sound reputation assists the school board through periods of painful decisions because the constituency trusts the members; a poor reputation intensifies the scorn or lack of confidence the general population has for its school board. When boards are realistic about their reputations in their communities, they are not distracted from governance by wanting to be "liked more." For those boards that do not hold the confidence or respect of their stakeholders, opportunities for engaged communication can improve the public reputation of the board in general.

The superintendent and district administration influence the school board. On rare occasions, this is negative. Mostly, school board members do not need to be educational professionals nor organizational professionals: They just need to keep their focus on a desirable future, govern accordingly, and let the high-level brain trust they have in their superintendent to take care of the details and watch as they influence the district. There are times, however, when the superintendent and school board do not agree. During these times, the administration will work hard to influence the board in its favor, but a wise board will discern its own decision.

The superintendent and his/her staff are experts trained to do precisely what is needed to build exceedingly successful schools, and this expertise is an important influence on school board decisions. Former educators sitting at the board table cannot replace this current expertise and must not assume they can. Leadership research has established a correlation between a healthy board and an effective senior administration, which directly affects student achievement through its direct relationship with schools. The district administration is highly influential and the board members must be strong governors and maintain their governance function.

UNIONS AND EDUCATION

The establishment of unions within education in the mid-1900s presented challenges and influences that have derailed many school boards from leading change and improvement. When unions and professional societies were introduced into education systems, school boards began to lose their confidence and comprehension of governance. The force of unions intimidated many school board members, who thought that their fundamental role had somehow changed with the introduction of labor negotiations. It had not.

Capitalizing on the 1950s human relations movement in organizations, teacher unions sought to infuse improved teacher welfare into the employer equation, which greatly influenced some board members, especially former teachers. In their intimidation, board members made decisions that caused them to be accused of being unfair or of wasting money. As a result of the ensuing collective agreements, there was a shift of focus from governing the learning environment for students to the workplace of teachers. The governance function requires that boards maintain balance over the entire learning system, and boards did not.

With the establishment of unions, school board members were also required to consider union requirements and expectations when developing district guidelines and the annual budget. In a rather unique response to the union presence, however, many school boards shifted their focus off of effective governance, including the careful stewardship of resources. These concessions weakened the role of the board in its leadership of the district, but should not have been a huge challenge in the context of sound governance.

Most boards did not recognize that governance can and must remain steadfast within the context of an increasingly unionized arena. Nor did they recognize that good governance also assures good labor relations.

BUREAUCRACY

The bureaucratic nature of school systems has also influenced the function of the school board. Bureaucracy has become the organizational form on which education rides. Some school board members have embraced their role at the 'top' of the bureaucratic hierarchy as justification for behaving as 'bosses' instead of governors, while others have simply been intimidated by the large and sometimes self-serving nature of a bureaucratic structure.

Larger school districts also introduced the dimension of bureaucratic complexity to governance, and this is where the challenge to community engagement emerged. Although bureaucracy has been an acceptable original form for service delivery across the public sector, in school systems it has intensified to the point that leadership of the school board is often benign. As a result, administrative ranks swelled and the impersonal rigidity of bureaucracy became evident in many school systems.

In the meanwhile, bureaucracy, with its impersonal rules, written records, hierarchy of command, and specialization of labor, has become the norm for most educational organizations, and has eroded the confidence of most school board members. Superintendents are required to relocate their expertise from supervision of schools to corporate administration, changing many recommendations brought to the board table. One of bureaucracy's harshest influences against good governance is that its rules and regulations, and hierarchy of permissions, can stand very firmly against community engagement.

It is ironic that the very structure that makes the delivery of education fair is also the structure that inhibits democratic engagement. Some brave school boards are pushing against the bureaucratic structure and have partnered with other levels of government and social services to provide a more holistic approach to the learning needs of students. The Australian Whole-of-Government movement has been applied to school systems in Kentucky, Saskatchewan, and Georgia, where innovative superintendents and boards have built asset-based school systems around the diverse needs of the students and the strengths of their educators.

Other school boards in central Canada and in North Carolina have implemented the core principles of community. In these situations, the structure of bureaucracy is being used to serve and advance the needs of learning rather than to maintain traditional and sometimes ineffective school policies and programs.

The complexity of education bureaucracy is intimidating, and has intimidated school board members so that few recognize that their primary role as representatives of local values and assets remains unchanged. Instead, it is commonplace for board members to become argumentative and antagonistic with community members, focused on defense of programs and policies, rather than offering oversight and foresight to the district.

In the context of bureaucratic influences, board members feel detached from schools and, as a result, in many ways feel less accountable for their decisions. They look at bureaucratic organization charts and see how many layers of administration separate them from the children, the classrooms, and the schools, and they feel ineffective. Without a clearer understanding of governance over hierarchical management, they interfere in levels well below the outlined duties of the board. However, when board members remain governors, they empower the employees of the district to serve in the strengths for which they were hired.

INFLUENCES OF CONFLICTS AND SERVICE DELIVERY

In its complexity, the modern school system is a complicated service organization balancing numerous needs and voices with varying demands and positions, and all of these can distract a board and influence its decisions away from sound governance. However, when board members are tightly focused on governance, these needs and service-oriented voices can help the school board to serve its students better. In service delivery, some of the core conflicts influencing school board decisions are easily recognized.

Most conflicts are either values conflicts or interest conflicts. This is also the case with conflicts regarding education services. Service delivery is often presented positionally, and quickly becomes adversarial. For example, the position of a group before the board might be more money for physical education, but the interest of the group is that the children need to be healthy, rested, and nourished so they can learn. The value conflict is that the children matter very much and their physical needs must be attended to!

Upon recognizing the interests behind the position, the board must meet the true need behind the request. In the example above, the board can respond to what is really being requested, perhaps in the form of breakfast programs or nutritional snacks for those students. Usually, when the interests of the request are understood, the board can respond with great success, even if it is not specifically more money for a particular program as presented in the original position.

School boards are also influenced by the public demands on schools. Today, schools are also expected to offer special learning supports that might include speech therapy, breakfast provision, career counseling, psychological and psychiatric counsel, health and safety training, advanced learning, second language training, English training, computer literacy, and the traditional "reading, writing, and arithmetic" of earlier generations. Many of these services do not fall within the traditional definitions of "school," yet many students need at least one of them. These are all valid influences on the board.

As an example of a values conflict, a school board that transfers its bussing contract from a local provider to an international school bus company reflects one of two values. Either the board does not represent a community that supports local business, or the board has made a decision that violates a local value. Each decision made at the school board table either reflects, rejects, or reinforces a local value, and so strengthens or erodes democratic local governance. It is the purpose of the school board to know which values and priorities are the most important to their communities and decide accordingly.

As the oversight body, the board has the final say on how services are delivered in broad terms. Some boards opt to contract out to private providers; some expand their administrations; others transfer or receive monies through other social service agencies. Importantly, though, it is the administration that administers service decisions! The form, or vehicle, should be a reflection of local values if the board is to govern well despite the complexities of services and the conflicts influencing them.

Another example of conflict might be the community desire for increased transportation in the context of a declining budget. Although school board members themselves do not need to provide solutions, they do need to maintain the vision of the community, and ask the district administration to offer recommendations. It is the task of the superintendent to determine an efficient and effective solution to fulfill that vision, and to present it to the board for its decision. Superintendents are well trained for these types of situations and must be free to pursue options without board interference. This is local governance.

THE INFLUENCES OF OTHER LEVELS OF GOVERNMENT

The school board's policy-making arena is frequently influenced by decisions made by other governments, either directly or indirectly. The decision to reduce or increase education funding, to change testing, to mandate daycare in school buildings, or even to amalgamate districts, are real-life examples of decisions imposed on school boards by senior governments that greatly influence the district and the board. Often these are difficult changes, and school boards are rarely consulted or provided with additional resources to incorporate legislated mandates.

During these more difficult periods of change, it is critical that the school board not be influenced away from its role as a conduit between the community and the district. During these periods, it is important that school board members tenaciously represent the assets, needs, and resources of the people the board represents. This is a vital governance role, but one that tends to fall away entirely when the influence of intense board meetings and decision-making demand much of the energy of board members.

When senior levels of government make demands of the school district, board members must be vigilant in remembering that their first obligation is to the public, and that their scope is education. Often during times of change, school boards forget to focus on education and get distracted in an effort to provide other services that are not within the role of the school district, but that help board members feel that they are still providing relevant leadership. The best thing boards can do at these times is to lead by staying on task and governing well!

Sometimes partisan politics influence the willingness of school board members to comply with the will of government. Some legislated policy directions do not fit comfortably with the board's direction, but others do. When policies have been initiated by duly elected officials, regardless of board members' own political views, they must be implemented. Legislation and regulations that affect school districts without consultation with the districts affected are a fact of modern life, and boards must learn to manage this reality effectively.

Governmental mandates can be readily accommodated within good governance, but pose a huge threat to poorly governed school boards. Poorly governed boards complain publicly about the threats to their authority, but this is a losing battle. School boards exist at the pleasure of the state. Rather than argue and complain, well-governed boards and districts roll up their sleeves and find a way to align the will of government with the priorities of the school district, so that the business of learning continues to take place effectively.

Without doubt, legislative decisions of senior governments will continue to challenge board members and influence school board decisions. Many school boards experience increased legislative control in the interests of cost-saving, rather than of student learning. Education should never be about saving money, but neither should education leadership ever waste money. But fiscal stewardship is a big part of board membership, and so board members often hear the mandate and focus on monetary savings, for example, rather than on student learning.

When there are budget cuts to be made, curiously, they usually come from the classroom. Rarely do boards ignore this recommendation and maintain their focus on learning. This is a curious behavior of school boards, but also one that speaks directly to the constituency, who often exercise their anger at the higher level of government responsible for the cuts in the first place. Well-governed boards need to govern during difficult times and make wise decisions, and not succumb to the temptation to use students and classroom educators as political fodder.

BALANCING THE INFLUENCE OF POWERFUL VOICES

When developing local education policy, board members are required to balance the opinions and mandates of parents and parent groups, legislation and regulations, unions, professional societies, interest groups, and even the powerful chief executive officer function within the superintendent's office. School board members are challenged by the cacophony vying for their focus. To be effective governors, they must forge through compelling and competing distractions to fulfill their mission of providing oversight of and insight into the district objectives, with student learning as the priority.

Boards that are easily influenced lose their student focus and further alienate themselves from those they serve and represent. They expect parents and professional educators to trust them and accept their policy direction and money-based decisions, but neglect the relationship required for such trust. Board members must always know where their constituency would be willing to compromise, and which matters are non-negotiable for them.

In successful organizations, including successful school boards, it is consistent focus and strong leadership that allows them to lead and thrive through difficult times.

PROFESSIONAL EDUCATORS

Professional educators are key contributors to school board policy, and their views are typically (but not always) provided through the voice of the superintendent. District leaders who ignore the concerns and attitudes of professional staff regarding student learning are not leaders, but neither should the lines of authority in the district be compromised by the school board. The opinions of teachers and other education professionals must matter to school board members, but in the interests of good governance, boards must provide an appropriate avenue for communication with these front-line professionals.

Teacher training and assessment has evolved so that modern classrooms are now staffed with university-educated professionals rather than the single, young, "school marm" of the last century. Educators bring fresh knowledge, research, and experience to policy discussions. Most school staffs include professionals who are not classroom-specific, yet are employed to facilitate the learning process for students. Together, education professionals also influence decisions undertaken by the school board.

BUSINESS PRINCIPLES AND THE PUBLIC SECTOR

In the late 1980s, initiated by Britain's Thatcher government and adopted in both the United States and Canada, the New Public Management movement applied business principles to the public sector, and influentially weaved its way into school board governance. With fiscal crises and the New Public Management movement overtaking many government organizations across the western world, demands for proven performance reached unprecedented levels, and school boards were influenced to find acceptable measures of district performance.

The performance measurement requirement associated with the New Public Management movement found a ready scapegoat in local school boards. While there were serious doubts about the will and capacity of school boards to provide effective leadership and governance, there were no mandated systemic reforms to the boards themselves. Wary of abolishing the immediate form of democracy represented by the local school board, senior governments decided instead to exercise their influence and diminish the responsibilities of the school board.

Pronouncing their lost confidence in local school boards, state leaders have wielded their political influence and reclaimed some of the core educational responsibilities that were delegated to school boards, including local taxation, how much students were required to learn (curriculum), and determined how this learning would be measured (standards testing).

The increasing challenges facing school board members to accurately reflect the views of those they represented justified interference from governments and furthered their application of New Public Management business principles to school districts. One of the critical challenges for school boards in this environment was that while the goals of government may be efficiency, effectiveness, and equality, the paramount goal of school districts is education. Measuring the outcomes of education in business terms is almost impossible, and challenged with defining realistic measures of success, school boards have struggled to demonstrate their relevance against the unfair influences of business principles applied to educational outcomes.

NON-GOVERNANCE RESULTS MEASURES

Based on another one of the fundamental principles of New Public Management, school boards were required by governments to demonstrate performance, and to compete for student numbers, funding, and general credibility based on their performance. Senior governments mandated standardized test results across North America in response to public demands for accountability. The mandate has been poorly received by teachers unions and by school systems in general, and complaints against "teaching to the test" have led the debates in education literature. For school boards, the challenges of this influence can still be answered by good governance.

In response to standardized tests, most boards have developed criteria that foray into management or operational areas rather than governance areas, and most certainly shift away from democratic engagement with local communities. Governance did not change with government-prescribed accountabilities, but this focus on how to test and measure caused board members to view their roles as more operational than governance.

Although many school boards today complain loudly about intrusions into their authority (and continue to complain in the media about loss of power to other levels of government), many focus their attention on the governance responsibilities left to them. Some school boards provide evidentiary support for their work, work hard to articulate the import of their role in democracy, and engage the support of their communities. A few engage their communities and work together to strengthen what is left, but the influences on school boards remain varied and strong.

THE CENTRAL ROLE IS UNCHANGED

Despite the increasingly complex and influential environment of education, and the apparent lack of confidence demonstrated by senior governments through micromanaging and intervention, there have been no significant reforms to the mandate or public selection of local school boards. After two centuries of school boards and numerous educational reforms, political authorities in North America still ultimately entrust the oversight of the delivery of education, and representation of the local voice, to elected school board members. This means that boards can stand for strong governance despite the influences.

For school board members and for those who are convinced that school boards could be impressive leaders, this represents great hope. The central role of school boards has not changed. With determination to authentically engage their communities, and to focus on strong governance through the leadership of relevant policy, school boards can provide well-run and well-equipped schools for our children, regardless of the influences.

According to voting patterns and candidacy numbers at election time, it would appear that school boards are perceived as increasingly irrelevant. Failure to lead decisively on the part of school board members will have grave consequences. More than ever in our history, citizens need democracy, and democracy needs an educated populace. Electing and supporting effective school board members will protect democracy.

DEMOCRATIC GOVERNMENT AT WORK THROUGH SCHOOL BOARDS

One of the primary influences of the school board is to demonstrate government at work. School boards demonstrate the three branches of democratic government when they are working, and this influences society. In North America, democratic governments have a legislative branch, an executive branch, and a judicial branch. School boards act as legislators when they develop the laws that govern the district. These local laws set policy, approve budgets, establish regulations, and engage constituents. In this way, school board members are performing a legislative function—when they are representing the people who elected them.

School board members perform an executive government function when they carry out policy. For a school board, this might mean approving the fee for an independent consultant in compliance with established policy, or approving a student field trip, or approving the appointment of principals, specialists, and even teachers, if policy requires board approval. This is a direct involvement in the administration of the district, and is ultimately an executive function. At the federal government level, these functions would not take place in the legislature; they would be part of a department function. They are combined at the school board level.

Finally, when all administrative avenues are exhausted, the school board remains the final body for appeal, and so the school board takes on a judicial function. This occurs when school boards make decisions regarding student expulsions, appeals, and evaluations of the superintendent. Thus, in the exercise of many of its regular duties, the school board embodies the three levels of government that make democracy unique from other systems.

Another important relationship between education and democracy is the teaching of skills and knowledge required to sustain a democratic state. Equal access to the common ability to read, write, and calculate is considered mandatory for the success and continuation of a strong economy and society. Even in 1786, Thomas Jefferson recognized that the diffusion of knowledge through common education was the surest foundation for the preservation of the freedom and happiness America cherishes. The school system, by its very structure, impresses the foundations of democracy on the young.

An additional important link between democracy and the work of school is the imparting of moral dispositions. These are the values that should be acceptable to all people in a democratic society—fairness, equality, justice, freedom, caring, community, and relatedness. The public purpose of schooling in a democratic society is also to impart those characteristic attitudes that cultivate the sense of self and of responsibility to a community. In recent years, this recognition has integrated many students of varied abilities and backgrounds into the same schools, so that they can learn together. Both reason and hope are sustained and nurtured in schools, when students learn and grow toward the common goals of our democratic state.

Finally, a school board is elected to protect and develop public education so that it will serve and improve democracy. This implicitly means that school boards must have an outward focus, which ultimately is their greatest influence. They must be mindful of the needs, capacities, and resources of their communities, and then ensure that the school system is developing to answer those needs.

There is a tendency for school systems to stand in the center of society and offer pre-established programs, rather than reaching outward to determine the needs of their communities and then asking the superintendent to change the district structure accordingly. This is partly a response to the bureaucratic nature of school systems, and the constraints of unionized employees, but it is not the appropriate role of the school board.

SUMMARY

The future of education lies ultimately within the decision-making practices of every elected school board member and their contributions at the board table. There are two influential paths for school board governance. School boards may determine to be what they were intended to be, as relevant, champion guardians of education, advancing the work of schools toward a future as diverse and incredible as the deepest dreams within each of us. Or, the school boards may continue toward obsolescence, jostled by the demands of competing interests and debilitated by members who allow themselves to lose their focus on strong governance.

School board members are still elected to guard the public trust and values, and to assure locally relevant policy to guide the school system, just as they were with the inception of school boards. It is here, in the fortitude of each elected school board member, that local boards can provide effective citizen leadership and governance to the American school system through the faithful execution of oversight, insight, and foresight within the complex arena of school board democracy. This is not hard work, but it does require fortitude, determination, and a clear understanding of purpose.

To press the views of the community into the schools, board members must *know*—not assume to know—what the views of their jurisdictions are. They must adopt a student-centered view of education, rather than an administrative or bureaucratic view. Only the board can do this. School boards can carefully develop the design of their governance model, and avoid the distractions of competing interests. Within strong governance, school board members are leaders who leverage the full potentials of the school system and the community to propel students confidently into their futures.

QUESTIONS

1. How do school boards protect democracy?
2. What are some of the influences that support good governance in your community?
3. What are some ways the school board might continue to govern well and interact with the community when other levels of government impose policies that do not align with local values or resources?

APPLICATION

Attend two consecutive school board meetings and while there, consider the many influences on your school board. Some will be governments, others will be organizations, some will be people, and some may be relationships. Draw a map identifying all of these and how they interact. From what you have observed at school board meetings, which ones are evidently most influential? What does the nature of the strongest influences tell you about the governing strength of your elected school board, and about who is truly leading?

THREE

Community Democracy

The Power of Engagement

One of the core and most compelling reasons for the establishment and continuation of school boards is the engagement of local democracy. Close examination of the practices of school boards (and for that matter, other levels of government) suggest there is a grave lack of understanding regarding what democratic engagement means. Most think immediately of voter turnout, but it is far more than that. This chapter will delve into the growing and persuasive field of community engagement, to suggest that it is through informed and intentional democratic engagement that school boards may make their greatest contributions.

Most school board reform literature suggests that the effective futures of school boards are to be realized through organizational restructuring, blurring the differences between education and business administration, changes to funding and funding formula, and short-sighted responses to the pressure of interest groups. None of these have been effective to date.

Grassroots democracy indicates that we are living in an era of community engagement. People desire to reengage with all levels of government, and this includes the school board. A community-engaged approach is democratic engagement in action, especially when guided by the school board. According to community-engagement literature, community members are co-investigators, co-educators, and more broadly, partners in addressing pressing community priorities. This is a highly relevant and important perspective, and one that school boards are uniquely structured to encourage and protect.

This does not mean that community members replace or even advise the educational professionals in the employ of the district. It does mean that the community can inform the board toward better policy development, because board members remain relevantly informed about issues and other important matters in the community that influence the school system. It also means that, as a result of an ongoing relationship and engagement with stakeholders as community members, the board's decisions reflect the will and values of the community.

Much of the literature about school boards and about governance incorporate an experts-based approach to local challenges, meaning that consultants and other experts are engaged to solve problems within and around the school district. However, answers can instead be found inside school district communities by seeking out the strengths, opinions, assets, and perspectives of the communities connected with the school system.

THE HISTORICAL ROOTS OF COMMUNITY ENGAGEMENT

Most North American citizens know that representative democracy insists that elected representatives properly serve the people they are elected to represent. Although trust in government at all levels is very low—a direct reflection of how poorly represented citizens feel by their elected officials—school boards can lead the change in this trend.

Thomas Jefferson, who conceptualized school boards for America in the late 1700s, contended that the cornerstone of our democracy rests on the foundation of an educated electorate. Jefferson was not just referring to formal schooling; he meant that for democracy to be representative, people needed to be engaged with democratic processes.

Almost a century after Jefferson, at the Soldiers' National Cemetery in Gettysburg, Pennsylvania, President Abraham Lincoln paraphrased theologian John Wycliffe with the oft-quoted vindication of democracy as "government of the people, by the people, for the people." These are foundational concepts in the United States and in Canada, announcing clearly that elected representatives must be an extension of the hearts and minds of the population. To do this, elected officials must be engaged with their communities.

WHAT IS COMMUNITY ENGAGEMENT?

Community engagement can be simply defined. It requires the participation of people in discussions of projects and issues that affect them. Focused on assets and capacity rather than need or deficiency, community engagement is a tangible way to approach the partnerships that school boards can form with their communities. Through engagement with their communities, school boards can draw on the resources available in the community to better focus on student learning (called school improvement in the older literature), and ensure that they have meaningful accountability measures in place for intentional results.

In fact, community engagement is so important for education that in 2014, the US Department of Education launched a framework to teach school and district staff how to engage with parents and the larger community to increase student achievement and build the type of effective community engagement that makes schools the centers of our communities.

Practicing democratic community engagement and establishing structural and institutional assurances for community engagement are initially difficult and time-consuming for school districts, but it is school board governance in action. According to the Carnegie Foundation website, community engagement describes the collaboration between education institutions and their larger communities (local, national, global) for the mutually beneficial exchange of knowledge and resources in a context of partnership and reciprocity. This is school board leadership!

Reciprocity is a core concept in community-engaged leadership. According to community engagement scholar Dr. Emily Janke of the University of North Carolina Greensboro, reciprocity is the recognition, respect, and valuing of the knowledge, perspective, and resources that each partner contributes to the collaboration. When school board members seek to consult and collaborate with their communities, reciprocity, defined this way, explains more fully what they are seeking to do. Effective community engagement is a lot of work, but for school board members, it can establish the kind of legacy that most people intend when they are elected.

PURPOSES AND PRINCIPLES

The purposes of community engagement are closely aligned with the purposes of the school board. The Carnegie Foundation has funded much research that is relevant to school boards. The website explains the purpose of community engagement, in part, as a partnership of knowledge and resources to enhance the tasks of school systems; to prepare educated, engaged citizens; to strengthen democratic values and civic responsibility; to address critical societal issues; and to contribute to the public good.

One of the important principles of community engagement is found in the distinction between cooperation and collaboration. School board members often refer to their partnerships with administration and with the citizens, students, and teachers they govern as collaborations or consultations. This is not accurate, and it is important for school board members to know the difference and to practice genuine collaboration in order for there to be authentic engagement.

In a cooperative or consultative setting the tone of the meeting is informing, based on the terms of reference "us," "them," and "they." In these meetings, which are very typical for school boards and their communities, the tone is listening, and terms like "we" and "our" are heard.which sound as though cooperationis taking place. It all seems very good. However, cooperative partnerships are not community-engaged partnerships. Cooperative partners meet irregularly, and people are contacted primarily through email or by telephone if there is a reason to meet. Intending to be collaborative, most school boards are actually cooperative, which works against the strengths and potentials of democratic engagement.

In contrast, collaborative partnerships engage their communities by meeting regularly and in person. The purpose of meeting is not to problem-solve; it is to build relationships. Cooperative partnerships emphasize coordination and maximize efficiency, independence, and autonomy. In subtle contrast, collaboratively engaged partnerships emphasize co-learning, power sharing, relationship building, and interdependence. Collaborative partnerships are much stronger and engaging in meaningful ways, especially for school boards.

In other words, democratic community engagement reflects values such as collaboration, participation, inclusiveness, reciprocity in public problem-solving, and equal respect for the knowledge and experiences that everyone contributes to education, to the generation of knowledge, and to community building. To truly engage with their communities, school boards need to shift from cooperative to collaborative leadership. They need to ensure that they are practically evidencing these values through policies that establish regular collaborative meetings.

COMMUNITY ASSETS

School boards are well positioned to lead the country in community-engaged policy development and community-engaged governance. Since community expertise often includes local financial institutions, fitness centers, independent businesses, the community club, local sports coaches, etc., collaboration with the communities of the school board provides access to great resources. These people have many types of knowledge and expertise that directly apply to the school board community. Sadly, these are often ignored or not even considered, and the views of experts external (and expensive) to the community are embraced instead.

One of the institutions of America best structured to preserve and promote democracy is the local school board. Consequently, elected school board members must engage the communities they represent in meaningful ways to ensure the continued freedoms of vibrant and vital democracy.

CONSULTATION AND COLLABORATION

Most school boards have some form of formal community consultation mechanism, but this is not typically meaningful, democratic, community engagement. Sadly, most consultations are usually public invitations to meet with board members in a time and place of the board's convenience. Whether or not the consultation is suitably timed and situated for the general population is not often considered, and some district board members just assume that all members of their community are aware of invitations to appear in front of the board.

All of these behaviors may be well intentioned, but they do not assure democratic or meaningful engagement. Such traditional strategies for improvement and for addressing challenges have often failed. This is, in part, because once the so-called "consultations" have taken place, many school board members convince themselves that low turnouts to consultations are an indication of community support for the work of the school board, rather than their lack of relationship with the community. In contrast, genuine community engagement takes effort and reflection.

Community engagement is about much more than formal meetings and numbers. Instead of focusing on needs and deficiencies, and of imagining public support without evidence, genuine community engagement discovers the capacities and assets of the community in order to meet challenges together.

In his writings about education, John Dewey argued compellingly that mere activity in a community does not constitute civic or democratic engagement. School boards pride themselves on their community activities, and many have policies that indicate a desire to be representative at the board table, but the question of how school boards are shaping the institutional structures of the district to definitively enhance a public culture of democracy is sorely lacking in evidence.

For school board members, the practice of community engagement combines the major goals of office: to be recognized by community members for sincerely soliciting their opinions, and to leverage their resources to ensure that the school district is indeed an extension of the communities it serves. In this way, community members can rethink their perceptions of the school system as a large and impersonal administrative bureaucracy with puppet board members, perceived to have little care or concern for the people that finance the system and support it with their children and grandchildren.

WHY IS COMMUNITY ENGAGEMENT RELEVANT TO TODAY'S SCHOOL BOARDS?

A community-engaged approach is relevant and important for school boards because the principles and practices invite the contributions of all stakeholders in the school system. John Dewey has had an immeasurable influence on modern education in America. One may recall that in his philosophy of education, Dewey maintained that school ought to be a reflection of real life, so that children came to school to learn to do things and to live in a community that gave them real, guided experiences. In turn, this fostered their capacity to contribute to society.

Although Dewey believed that students should be involved in real-life tasks and challenges, for some reason, school boards have departed from these central principles and look to experts to resolve the tasks and challenges they confront. Community engagement is relevant for today's school boards because it reestablishes the purposes of schools in the school board governance model.

THE BENEFITS OF ENGAGING THE COMMUNITY

Community engagement is also important because it emphasizes and draws on specific knowledge, frameworks, skills, and techniques of formal training contributed by community members and stakeholders. Additionally, community engagement is relevant for today's school boards because it places effective change within the capabilities of those who will be most affected by the changes contemplated at the board table.

School boards that intentionally engage their communities meaningfully and purposefully include members of the general public in educational political processes. This restores the democratic spirit and enriches and empowers the partnership between the school board, those it governs, and those it represents.

EMPOWERMENT

Discussions of empowerment permeate the literature of education, and school boards have an important role to play in ensuring that people associated with their school districts are empowered. This is directly associated with community engagement.

School boards may not be able to control their fiscal incomes, but they do have the authority to establish structures that empower individuals to contribute significantly to achieving the goals of the district. School boards have rich resources in parents, educators, administrators, students, and other engaged citizens.

Empowerment puts particular groups of people at the center and views them as important resources, rather than as a problem. In this way, when school boards take the time to engage and empower members of the school district community, the people they represent can recognize that their board members really do represent them and their interests, and that the board members are accountable to their community.

An empowering approach to engaging school district communities builds on a number of qualities that are affirming for people and that boost the confidence of the public in their school board members. Different people have knowledge, skills, values, initiatives, and motivations to solve problems that can greatly assist the work of school boards. Although there are some different meanings for empowerment in different contexts, for the most part, empowerment connotes many positive things, like choice, dignity, recognition of values, control, and capability. When these qualities are sought by school board members looking to leverage these strengths for the benefits of the district, only positive outcomes result.

Empowered and engaged communities are a tremendous strength to school boards, and they ensure connections between the board and the district. In 2002, the World Bank identified four key elements of empowerment that occur across social and political contexts. These are useful guidelines for school boards seeking to improve community empowerment within their districts:

- Access to information
- Inclusion and participation
- Accountability
- Strength within the organization

These four elements of empowerment provide pathways to community engagement, but they also provide building blocks for community-engaged policy development, both of which are explored in the following pages.

ACCESS TO A WEALTH OF INFORMATION

Sufficient access to information is such a critical part of the democratic process that there is now legislation in Canada and the United States that protects and supports the rights of the citizenry to information used in the development of public policy. By extension, this means that access to information that has guided school board decision-making is a critical part of school board governance.

School boards can ensure they are providing adequate access to their decision-making processes in simple ways like understandable minutes, holding very few "in camera" sessions, and by engaging their communities consistently regarding matters that are important enough for the community that they are elevated for consideration to the school board table.

One of the consistent criticisms of school boards in media is secrecy and closed door meetings, which is exclusionary in practice and infuriating to the electorate. Access to information empowers and engages the district community. Sharing appropriate information with the community as a school board assures school board members that they are working with and for their constituency.

INCLUSION AND PARTICIPATION

Surprisingly, school boards are like many democratic bodies, and operate in an exclusionary manner with much more ease than they do as inclusive bodies that encourage participation. This is a fairly simple response to bureaucratic and policy-based governance and the need to protect privacies, but it does not need to be characteristic of good school boards.

One of the simpler ways to assure inclusion and participation is to establish them in the structure of the district through the revision of existing board governance policies and the development of specific policies that prohibit disingenuous behaviors while entrenching sincere inclusion and participation. In other words, inclusionary, participatory policy processes are pathways to community engagement. They also promote access to information, accountability, and the capacity of the local organization to excel in its work.

COMMUNITY ENGAGEMENT STRENGTHENS THE ORGANIZATION

"Building capacity" is a term that has gained much traction in matters of organizational reform, but for the school board member or the community member, it simply speaks to maximizing the potential and strengths within the organization of the school district. This is the core of community engagement and one of the ways that increased capacity is leveraged and maximized by the school district.

In a world of bureaucracy, we tend to think that building capacity in organizations means more rules and accountability, but what it really means is a culture of confidence and collaboration, in which everyone affected by the district feels they make an important contribution—and as a result, they do! Curiously, those organizations with maximized capacity do not have issues with sick leaves, attrition, grievances, and disenfranchised voters. While community-engaged governance results in increased local organizational capacity, it is also the pathway through which the capacity of the organization is increased.

Growing research about community engagement explains the four critical pathways to community engagement described above. Each of these pathways provides school boards with specific and relevant areas of resources that can meaningfully inform their work. In democratic community engagement, the level and type of involvement of people changes over time, according to phase, activity, purpose, and members, but the engagement piece steadily gains strength. It is a model that can embed deeply into a community and inform school board members meaningfully long after the original implementation of community-engaged principles and policies.

COMMUNITY ENGAGEMENT AND POLICY DEVELOPMENT

School boards develop policy, and in modern times, more and more school boards, like other levels of government, are embracing the wisdom of community engagement in policy development. One simple reason why community-engaged policies and policy development are smart for school boards is because they significantly reduce conflict! There is broad literature available about policy development and policy cycles, so further discussion is not necessary here.

For the purposes of this chapter and for general governance wisdom, school boards ought to ensure that everyone who will be affected by a policy be involved in the development of that policy. This takes a lot of time, and often requires skills of facilitation and even mediation. In the end, the result is well worth the effort of meaningful inclusion in policy development.

Of course, board members can delegate physical involvement in the policy work, but then they must be certain that participants understand that members of the board are engaged partners in the process, regardless of their physical presence. It is appropriate for board members to be present when the policy process directly involves the community, and often inappropriate for them to be present during the discussions of internal policies and regulations.

There is an important trend in board governance to distinguish between policies of the board (which are governance-focused), and policies of the district administration (which are usually rules and regulations that flow from the policies of the board). This means simply that when board policies are under development or review, board members engage with their community under the leadership of the board chair. When the rules and regulations of a well-run school district are under review, employees are engaged in the process under the leadership of the superintendency.

COMMUNITY-ENGAGED PRACTICES

A quick scan of the websites of most public organizations, including school boards, indicates a desire, at least at the official level, to effectively exercise community-engaged practices. However, it takes much time and effort to establish community-engaged policies that result in democratic, community-engaged practices.

It takes little time and effort to craft words that sound good but that, in fact, do not hold the district, its administration, or its board in any way accountable or responsible to engage the community on issues and practices that affect them. Sadly, the official-sounding community engagement policies are more the truthful reality than actual, meaningful engagement.

People run for office and are elected with a sincere (we hope!) desire to serve meaningfully and to represent fairly, but as the vast literature about organizational reform, school board reform, leadership, and organizational capacity informs us, elected officials who do engage their communities are the exception, not the norm. Even in our intentions toward meaningful community engagement, we defer to the experts and authorities rather than the grassroots to determine how best to proceed.

Community-engaged practices are easy to recognize by the lack of evidence! Community-engaged boards have positive relationships with their communities, and this is most readily recognized in the opinion of the general public about the school board and about the schools.

While no organization exists without its critics, community-engaged school boards are part of a synergistic relationship with the people they serve and represent. In school districts governed this way, decisions are made collaboratively, employees speak well of the board, there is an effective, trust-based relationship between the board and the senior administration, and conflict is transformed rather than avoided. These boards usually have very small, relevant board policy manuals that are reviewed on a regular and systematic cycle, and board members do not hide from their public behind paper, policies, and process.

In short, members of community-engaged school boards feel a loyalty and respect for the people they serve, and it shows in the way they govern the school district and interact with members of the community. Their focus is on the assets within the community, rather than relying on experts to discern and provide resources and policies.

Within the community are appropriate responses to the many issues our students, educators, and neighborhoods are challenged with today, including vandalism, bullying, budget cuts, racism, poverty, and the constant flow of policy changes in response to legislative mandates at regional and national levels. In many ways, community engagement is a civic sentiment that cannot be captured in policies and procedures. Instead, community-engaged policies and procedures are the result of a school board that practices community-engaged governance, ensuring that they are relevant, appropriate, respectful, and respected.

GOOD GOVERNANCE AND COMMUNITY ENGAGEMENT

The relevance of relationship-driven community engagement to good governance speaks to the heart of the school board. By governing with an engaged community, the school board can facilitate the release of individual and group capacities, which in turn strengthens and mobilizes local economies and locally based community development.

The focus of community engagement suggests that focusing on the needs, problems, and deficiencies of a community does not energize or renew a community, yet this is often the starting point for school boards, especially at budget time or when confronted with difficult decisions as a result of fiscal constraints. The community-building capacities of community engagement can ensure that any school district can enjoy maximized potential, and be relevant to and representative of its community for the benefit of the schools within the district it governs.

According to community-engagement literature, inherent within each community is a unique combination of assets upon which the future may be constructed. Although many school board members concur with this philosophy, it is simpler to follow the lead of others at the board table, and the lead of private-sector management styles, and pay external consultants for assistance.

To access the assets within a community, school boards must undertake the process of locating the assets, skills, and capacities of residents, of community groups, and of community institutions. Local banks, department stores, libraries, police, and hospitals are examples of community institutions that are particularly skilled at integrating and leveraging the assets and relationships required to build the communities they serve.

There are also groups of people that voluntarily come together to solve problems, and these are usually cultural and/or church groups. Such local organizations can add tremendous strength to assist school boards in identifying community capacities and assets, and in resolving the challenges of modern school board governance.

In their seminal work on asset-based community engagement, *Building Communities from the Inside Out: A Path Toward Finding and Mobilizing a Community's Assets*, Dr. John Kretzmann and Dr. John McKnight identified and explained how to mobilize an entire community to refocus and regenerate it. Although this is time-consuming and intense work, it mobilizes communities around vision and develops plans accordingly. School boards can be community leaders in this way.

COMMUNITY-ENGAGED SCHOOL BOARD LEADERSHIP

There are many stories of great success involving school boards that govern with democratic engagement through community-engaged leadership and asset-based development.

One district in central Canada encountered challenges that included complicated funding formulas, segregated communities, and underutilized resources. Ultimately, the survival of the district was at threat because the communities themselves were faced with a slow but steady demise due to an urbanization focus of the provincial government and serious natural challenges to the largely agrarian area.

While refusing to collapse, the school board faced almost impossible odds of survival in their remote rural area. Some of their schools, built to house more than five hundred students, hosted eight to twenty students in one academic year after another. Meanwhile, economic downturns and state policies that encouraged urbanization continued to threaten not just the district, but the livelihood of the many families living in the community.

As entire towns collapsed, the school board hired a superintendent's team of two women who embarked on a project of "reimaging" their district, and engaged the entire community, anyone connected in any way with the school district, in the process. In 2014, the district was a finalist for an award of excellence for its relevant and innovative governance and administration. The school district continues to thrive in the strength of their engaged communities, despite discouraging and ongoing fiscal challenges.

SUMMARY

This chapter has explored the power and strength of community engagement. As a core democratic principle, community-engaged governance means that school boards are collaborative. They maintain ongoing, positive interactions and relationships with the people of their communities and all the stakeholders of the school system. When school board members employ relationships of reciprocity, strengths and assets flow from the community to the school board. This greatly informs the board members and assures them that when the board makes decisions, including difficult decisions, members are working with, rather than against, their community.

In a democratic state, community engagement is tangible evidence of the unique strengths and role of the school board in action. Respectful and trusted relationships, reciprocity, collaboration, engagement, enthusiasm, meaningful policies, and asset-based decision-making are all evidence of community-engaged school boards. It is this capacity to work synergistically with all facets of the community that sets a community-engaged school board apart from a problem-based school board, and demonstrates the original vision for school boards in America.

QUESTIONS

1. What are the key evidences of community engagement?
2. What are the challenges to community engagement for your local school district and board?
3. What challenges in your community could be addressed with the asset-based approach of democratic community engagement?

APPLICATION

This is a community-engagement exercise. Pretend that an old school, but one that has been in use, has been completely destroyed by fire. No one was hurt, but it has caused great upset in the community, and the school board members know that people in the community are angry. They blame the board for not replacing the school several years ago, when they had the opportunity. Make a chart identifying the partnerships of people, groups, and businesses that comprise this school district community. Next, with these partnerships in mind, plan a community event that would engage the community and improve the relationship with the school board. Which principles would you use to guide your plans, and how would they influence how you contact people? What questions would you ask at the event? What would you do to ensure that people were truly engaged? How would you know that you had achieved your goals?

FOUR

Governing Democracy

The Politics of Education

According to Aristotle, politics is simply described as who gets what, when and how. This description references the distribution of resources, and seems crude when applied to the work of schools or to the many facets comprising the business of learning. But, in fact, school boards are political bodies that make political decisions; they influence administrative decisions through the governance policies they establish and uphold.

In this way, school boards create and resolve conflict in their resource allocation processes. This is the politics of education. The primary example of resource allocation is the budget process, when board members determine the general categories for fiscal investment. Political decisions are also made when board members implement teacher evaluation policies, interdistrict policies, and even fund-raising policies at the district level.

Every decision the board makes distributes public resources at a particular time in a particular fashion. The politicization of school boards in this way is a positive aspect of democratic engagement. However, when the politicization of school boards becomes partisan, board members follow the principles of their political party, not the best interests of the community. It is important for community members to recognize board members whose loyalty is to their political party more than to the community they represent.

Politics in education is about the administration and control of a school district. School board members are elected to oversee the administration and control of the district. They are politicians, and we expect that board members, like other elected governors, will ensure that the area we have entrusted to their stewardship will be run well and responsibly.

However, the administration of the day-to-day activities is the responsibility of the superintendent, not the school board or any individual school board member.

The superintendent is the board's most valued asset. This office requires both an educational expert and a sophisticated administrator. The political obligation of the board is to ensure that he or she is doing the job reasonably. When the superintendent is not, the annual evaluation is the appropriate forum to address such concerns.

It must be absolutely clear to board members and to the voting public that the board does not perform the work of the superintendent, and that the superintendent is the employee of the board. Citizens unhappy with the district put pressure on the board, which in turn pressures the superintendent for explanations.

Dissatisfaction with the work of the superintendent is within the exclusive domain of the board. Boards controlled by their employees are boards that have lost their political influence and no longer function as governors. Consistent and meaningful engagement with the community is a democratic means of protecting the board and the community from a superintendent who runs the district in his or her own interests.

Some of the confusion regarding the work of school boards may be rooted in the fact that there is not really a common forum for learning about governing, which is another central purpose for this book. Most of us exercise our right to vote, but that is our only involvement with politics. We believe in democracy, but research has shown that for most of us, democracy means majority rule.

Democracy offers citizens the privilege of choosing their government, or its leadership. If we truly understood the connection between education and democracy, or how important the work of school board is, more of us would run for office, and many more of us would vote. Perhaps the responsibility for the detachment of our school boards has as much to do with our inability to articulate the value of politics to education as it does with confusion about the role of school board members.

For example, only a few university politics departments teach about education policy; fewer faculties of education teach about school board governance. Since there is a recognizable void in the understanding of the voting public and others in terms of the work and politics of the school board, it should come as little surprise that most people do not understand what school boards do, or how they do it.

Finally, politics involves accountability and transparent communication. When public resources are distributed, the public is entitled to understand value. School board members should be able to account for the progress of the district in terms that everyone can understand. We would all be extremely well served to be able to hear of concrete school district results, apart from student achievement. Typically we do not.

Without infringing in any way on the restrictions of collective agreements and union codes, a school board could communicate its achievements similarly. We could hear that 6,000 students are acquiring an additional language, and that 1,300 have reached a particular proficiency level in music. We could also learn that 900 students were removed from the district by their parents, or that 900 new ones registered.

By engaging in regular dialogue with the public, school boards can know what to communicate regarding their leadership. For some boards, public accounting could mean disclosing the number of dollars spent on corporate lunches, board member travel expenses, hotel costs for retreats, etc. In this way, the politics of spending would provide accountability.

There is much to celebrate in a school district, and politics asks that school boards tell us what that is, but to be genuine. False celebrity is deceitful and insulting. Democratic politics asks that community engagement be the vehicle to assure that end. Merely recording selected information into a newsletter for some parents, holding occasional "consultations," and writing policies that promise but do not practice community engagement are not enough.

The entire population funds schools with tax dollars; the entire population should be champions for our school districts. As the leadership of the district, the school board is the most likely candidate to facilitate the enthusiastic engagement and support of the public. Accountability for public service should never be avoided. School boards are obligated to evidence their track records clearly for public evaluation.

COMPLAINTS

School board members are magnets for complaints, but this is not the negative occurrence that many consider it to be, and is an indication that people want to be meaningfully involved in the school district. Board members need to recognize that just as they are not elected to run the school system, they are also not elected to solve all of its problems. However, complaints can be very good tools for better governance and provide the board with opportunities to communicate the value of the school system's work to the public; they also provide the potential for greater community engagement and for a revised vision.

Complaints are good; they lead to a new vision. People who complain about the school system are usually very passionate. Each trip to the grocery store, the local rink, the beach, or the park is an opportunity for board members to meet a constituent and chat with them, and most importantly, to listen.

When a complaint is communicated to the board, school board members can use the complaint to fuel a better vision for the school district. Complaints usually reveal some area where constituents feel they are not receiving value for their money. Often these represent an opportunity for improved communication and for further engagement with the community; on rare occasions, they are a signal that something is very wrong. School board members can be important ambassadors for change in this regard, and by listening to the complaint, can identify areas that they, as governors, should be auditing.

There is a cultural tendency in some school districts to ignore any and all complaints and "celebrate" only the good things in the district. Complaints should never pose a threat to the leadership of the district; they are opportunities for improved service. Interestingly, when school boards regularly engage with their communities, complaints are rarely received, and instead become parts of ongoing discussions during the regular, planned encounters with the community.

Most complaints need to be resolved through the level at which there is a concern. For example, staff problems (except problems with the superintendent) are not resolvable by the board. These need to be handled through the school, or at least through the superintendent, because district employees report to the superintendent.

Board members must never communicate directly with the superintendent's employees about a complaint—they must go through the superintendent, as he or she is their sole contact, usually clearly stated in policy, with the rest of the district. As an example, how can the board hold the superintendent accountable for his or her leadership if board members are interfering with personnel matters and making decisions that do not exhibit good and wise governorship?

THE VALUE OF COMPLAINTS

Sometimes complaints are simply complaints. When board members listen carefully to the views of constituents or to groups of constituents, some "complaints" are indications either of areas the board is neglecting or of new areas the board might want to explore. Examples might be widely expressed concerns over administrative spending on office equipment, lack of academic achievement, a missing music program, or even frequent staff turnover.

When listening to a constituent, the board or board member must consider the validity of the complaint. When it comes to complaints about taxation, the complainers may not recognize the personal opportunity they have to invest in young people, the future leaders of the world. Perhaps this should be viewed as an alert to the board. The board needs to review or renew the efforts to communicate its purposes and accomplishments to the people that fund the system in ways that those investors regard as valuable.

Often people whose children are not currently in the school system are convinced that they should not have to pay for education through their taxes. For example, one of the most frequent complaints board members hear is about the cost of public education. People are simply saying that they do not see value for their money.

Interestingly, even in their own budget processes, board members themselves may communicate this message to their administrations. Board members jump on small details within proposed budgets, and force the administration to defend what are usually minor proposals in the context of the full budget. The board, too, is searching for genuine evidence of value.

It is the responsibility of the board to ensure that the people who contribute resources and children to the school system are confident that their elected members are good stewards of those resources. The board must work with the community and the superintendent to ensure that the work of the school system is integrated with and reflects the values of the community.

WHEN THE PUBLIC DISAGREES WITH SPENDING DECISIONS

Some concerns over district spending are valid, and board members must be carefully tuned to recognize when legitimate spending for student needs crosses into wasteful spending by senior members of the district. For a board that hears this complaint often, they might want to consider a vision that guarantees money is directly benefiting students. Again, this offers two opportunities: one for building trust and a new vision; and one for appearing and being foolish.

Some board members claim that any expenditure ultimately benefits students (expensive lunches for district administrators helps them develop a more harmonious team; higher salaries for school board members allow them to devote more time to the district; leather couches for school district office staff make them feel valued), and so boards disregard the queries of those who pay the bills.

Other board members establish visions that allow budgets to be built from the classroom out, so that when money is tight, the classrooms are not doing without. Board members build reputations based on how they and the rest of the board receive complaints. Responses are entirely at the discretion of the elected board. Regardless, complaints are always opportunities for improved relationships and for increased communication between the board and its constituency.

Other times, the board may hear complaints from angry or disappointed citizens, which offers it a rare opportunity to champion a cause together with its constituency, and strengthen levels of understanding, trust, and respect.

CAUGHT BETWEEN GOVERNMENT AND COMMUNITY

There are times, though, when the board must navigate difficult decisions. There are no simple answers in these situations, but good boards will weather these difficulties together with their communities, and both will be strengthened as a result. Often, however, the opposite happens. Conflict is difficult, and it is often particularly difficult for school board members, who have no individual authority and must act as a collective.

Consider, for example, the widespread public request for a neighborhood high school in a relatively new subdivision quite a distance from any other district schools. In this scenario, the board and administration both recognize the need for another building based on student population projections. There are also logistical challenges to sending students via a complicated public transit route to other district high schools, miles away, both maximized with student populations already. In this situation, it is the state government that has refused the request, claiming that there is space in the schools of other districts within the same city. It is an impossible situation.

Some boards would be defeated and discouraged by the position of the government and struggle against their communities to try to explain the position of the government. This would turn hostilities toward the board members. Some boards might ask their local school board association to petition government on their behalf, but this is likely not to bring the desired results, and the board members themselves would not be seen to be working hard for their students or ratepayers.

Other boards would recognize that if senior governments want to involve themselves in prohibiting the locally determined best solution to advance better education for students, then they can be asked to offer other solutions. As publicly elected representatives, the board members would petition government with letters, phone calls, and even the full presence of all board members and interested constituents at the state legislature.

This is obviously not a problem a board can solve on its own, so board members must seize the opportunity to partner with the people they represent to leverage the will of the legislature on behalf of students and their families. In this scenario, a widespread complaint offers the potential for a strengthened partnership between the board and its community. School boards also exist to ensure efficient and equitable distribution of resources, and they must work with their community to find the balance.

These days there are often not enough dollars in the public coffers to meet all the demands being placed on schools, and board members must choose between priorities. Communities expect their schools to be fully equipped service centers, offering a broad range of programs, but are typically reluctant to pay increased fees for such schools. This is another opportunity for board members to be certain that they are a genuine liaison between the community and the school system. When this happens, difficult budgetary decisions can be made in collaboration with the schools and the community. The result is usually something everyone can live with.

THE WRONG RESPONSE

Unfortunately, there are always board members who think they alone can change the distribution of public dollars, and they may even bully other board members to get their way. Accurate communication by conscientious board members can ensure that their public understands their work and contributions to the district, and the restrictions placed on each board member through the democratic parameters of board governance.

Some communities elect a board candidate who makes promises directly to them. Voters unfamiliar with good board governance think that one board member will have the power required to redirect the school division in favor of their election promises. This is incorrect: It is a governing board that registers a majority vote for each of its decisions.

Rarely does one individual have enough influence to sway an entire board in a direction that does not uphold district goals, but it happens more than one may expect. This is complicated by the fact that voters may elect their school board members without an understanding of board governance, and so they live for decades with a school board that does not serve education well, and continue to elect members who may be benign or even harmful to the health of the organization.

There is tremendous challenge for school boards in reconciling the diverse and often conflicting expectations of their communities, especially when the electorate does not understand how boards govern. Board members must always ensure that the board's policies and decisions reflect the broader interests of the entire community they serve, and that these decisions move the district closer to achieving stated goals.

This is much easier when the school district is established to focus outward instead of inward, and not preoccupied with preserving the interests of the people within the structure. When making decisions at the board table, members must be very mindful that they are acting in the interests of all students, employees, and citizens, for the betterment of everyone in the schools. Only the elected board members bring this unique perspective to the table.

Those who view themselves as rubber stamps for administrative demands fail the constituency they represent. These board members are in constant tension with their communities. Just as all relationships require effort and understanding to succeed, so the school board must expend effort and understanding when learning how to reconcile diverse community representation with the recommendations of the education administration.

INVESTMENT

There is much value in education. Huge public dollars are invested in educating our young. Recognizing complaints as opportunities for audit, or as keys to a new vision, or even as an effective method to develop constituency relationships, benefits the work of the board and helps the public shift its thinking away from costs toward the notion of the common investment we all make in education.

Boards are the leadership link between public trust and the sophisticated school systems of today. Schools are well served by board members who actively govern with integrity, knowledge, vision, and wisdom. When these board members conduct their elected roles properly, there is rarely debate in public forums or in private corners about the lack of value of public education.

THE ROLE OF BOARD MEMBERS

American school board members are remarkable in their sincere desire to influence school systems for the benefit of children. Enthusiastic, passionate people eager to improve the school system are necessary on our school boards. Each board member can bring hopes and desires for change to the table, but it is the collective will that must lead the district. School board members must pause and ponder several aspects of the environment into which they have been elected, so they can determine what their personal contributions can be.

Misunderstanding the work of the school board has resulted in a lack of clarity around the purpose of the school board member and the resultant misunderstanding of the role of the school board. Board members need to be vigilant in assisting their communities to understand their role—once they are clear on what that role is. Many well-meaning but obstinate school board members have damaged the work of the board and the school system it governs by assuming their own ideas of governance are correct, although they have not learned it from any authority.

Good governance is not inherent; people do not suddenly acquire the skills of good governance when they are elected to the school board. Governance is a specific role, and one that the school board must fulfill. Board members must learn to govern. Good school board governance is not taught anywhere but in the context of board governance, and for most school board members, even then training is optional. When board members understand governance, future candidates for the school board gain a clearer understanding of governance, and the entire district benefits when they are elected.

The role of the school board is not as complicated as modern practice would have us believe. For many of the reasons and evolutions in education cited earlier, board members are unclear on what makes a good school board, while people not on the school board give school boards little thought. Boards require consensus (decisions everyone can live with), they require initiatives that will improve schooling, and they need to be able to communicate the values of the community to the school district, so that the district reflects local values. School boards provide oversight, insight, and foresight. They do not micromanage. The mandate is quite simple.

The purpose of the school board has not changed since its inception. There are so many factors interacting within school districts that board members are often lured off their role and lose track of their purpose of ensuring a well-run district. Depending on events in the district and trends in education at the time, board members can be thrust into their new positions with little or no training. There are some steps that help new board members and people interested in school boards to recognize the working purpose of the school board.

SIMPLE STEPS TO AVOID CONFLICT

Taking the time to understand the intentions of the preceding board and the superintendent improves the contributions of the school board member toward governance, and avoids conflicts in many ways. Learning about the track record of the previous boards will allow the new school board member to better understand the current circumstances of the district. Those who do not take the time to pause and reflect can hinder the district and frustrate fellow board members, and even undo some good work that has taken place before.

Often a comprehensive view of what is happening in the district can provide the board member with greater insight into areas that need to be brought to the attention of the collective board. This record should be clearly evident by reading the board minutes from several years prior. Board members typically do not want to hinder the important work of education, and so taking time to become familiar with the board record, goals, steps toward its goals, and other prior achievements is time well invested.

Taking the time to pause and understand the district vision and culture is essential to attainment of the goal of a positive future, and also prevents some conflicts. For example, school board members really need to understand the vision of the school district in which they serve. Although visions are scribed by the board, there is usually one in place when the board is elected. The vision must be clear, and it is intended to guide decision-making. It should also be evident all over the district, and especially among the board members.

The vision should be a visceral response: When people "feel" the vision, they are willing to work hard and be involved. When new board members cannot share the vision or see it in action, they cannot support it. This means that either the vision must be reestablished, or a new one determined. This is part of guarding the public trust and represents a vital contribution by the new board member. Misunderstanding the vision of the district is also a source of conflict that can be easily avoided.

Some conflict comes from visions that are nice words that cannot be embraced or evidenced by the district personnel. When this happens the board has a leadership problem, because the vision is not guiding district behavior. If the stated vision is not guiding the work, spending, and other decisions of the district, what is? Obscure visions make work difficult for everyone.

A clear vision is leadership. Board members must lead through the establishment of a vision everyone can enthusiastically support, and can determine this vision by understanding their communities and consolidating those education values into the district vision. Typically, such a vision is birthed through consistent and meaningful engagement with the communities of the school district.

In its broadest terms, the vision of all school boards is an improved future, though this is not a very exciting term, and so we rarely read it as a stated vision. On one hand, we want the same results, but localized and improved: We want a better school experience and performance every day. In reality, people are not motivated to work hard, work extra, and carry the torch for an "improved future."

Boards try to find motivational words for their visions because they are sincere about making a difference, but in fact, their policies can guide the actions of everyone in the school system, adding strength and power to the improved future the school board members are elected to protect. Through engaged interaction with community, which in turn informs the policy process, board members can ensure that the school system is not just meeting needs, but accomplishing what is needed. This is usually the intent behind the sentimental, noble, or extremely long vision statements characteristic of school boards.

Fancy statements do not really reflect leadership and do not guide daily activity. Board members, like anyone else working in the school district, should be able to state the vision concisely and precisely, so that in the few words, everyone may understand how they can contribute, what the common goal is, and when that vision has been achieved.

If the district and the community could articulate their own clear vision to guide the district in response to the community around them, school boards would be obsolete in this area. Some are, but not by design.

Most districts and communities look to their governing school boards to define the vision of education they pursue. Visions also attract or discourage potential district personnel, and so must be mindfully established. The vision is broadly a better future version of our democracy, expressed in educational terms.

THE SCHOOL BOARD AND THE VISION

School board members must set and also embrace their district's vision, champion the direction the district is headed, and then, as a board, resource and monitor the district so that the vision is achieved. Consider these actual vision statements: "Creating new learning opportunities each and every day" is much more motivating and achievable than "Inspiring potential." Some districts have forty-five-word vision statements (one in northern Canada, for example), which are irrelevant.

Meanwhile, statements like "The learner is the focus of all we do" gives a clear message to everyone in the school system—from the student, to the teachers, to the ratepayers, and even to the school board members. People in this school district know why they get up in the morning, and even taxpayers with little engagement with the schools can participate in this vision, and they can understand school board decisions at a broad level.

The school board and the school district, together with the community, can champion the important work they do. It is highly likely that this kind of district school board does not field many complaints about the cost of education, or questions regarding its value. The entire community knows how resources are being invested, and are active participants in setting those priorities.

Another attribute of the local school board member is the fact that he/she is *not* required to be a professional educator or a professional education administrator. According to Thomas Jefferson, the great strength of the school board is the perspective of the lay person: Community members are intended to be experts in community liaison, not in education, so that their role is to press local values into the programs and policies of the school district.

School board members should be able to influence the school district when it is alienating or frustrating the community it serves, and lead the district back on track. Times have changed, but the original purposes of education remain, and community engagement remains the best vehicle for school board governance. Schools teach children how to learn. Board members make sure the values of the community are reflected through district operations.

DRIFTING FROM LOCAL VALUES

Thomas Jefferson's elaborate plan to make education available to every person has evolved into large corporate entities that govern and administrate much larger, specialized schools in comparatively huge geographical areas. As school systems become increasingly large and sophisticated, and as educational professionals and interest groups exert pressure on the school system, the potential to ignore the students, or even eliminate local values, becomes a genuine threat to the intended democratic purposes of the school board.

School board members must be vigilant and courageous when sifting through the persuasions of interest groups, and remember that it is the learning environment that they are elected to govern. At the base of these complex hierarchies, as far removed from the school board as possible in a bureaucratic structure, are the students—the central purpose of the school system!

The original purpose of the school board has not changed, but the context in which education is delivered is radically different. The school board member is elected to guard the public trust by setting goals, and then to lead the school district toward fulfillment of those educational goals deemed valuable by law and by the communities they serve. These days there are many interests and stakeholders arguing that they are best able to describe the will and best interests of society—but this role has been delegated through legislation to the local school board.

It is hard to keep the focus on the child while maintaining an oversight role. It is critical that, in the pressure and importance of government, school board members stop regularly and ask themselves how—or if—their decisions will directly improve learning. The voting record of the school board should demonstrate a decisive path toward a specific vision that concretely improves education.

THE POLITICS OF PUBLIC TAX DOLLARS

There are very sound historical—and practical—reasons for the public financing of school, yet opinions regarding public taxation are among the largest issues school board members encounter. Education is an investment and a gift that benefits all of society. It equalizes us. There is a common theme through most of Thomas Jefferson's writings, and so throughout the founding documents of America, that pleads for the rightful place of education in a self-governing society.

Jefferson pioneered the establishment of the American education system on the firm belief that members of society must look after one another, and that elected school boards must help their constituencies shift their thinking from expense to investment with regard to education financing, and help the public understand the tremendous social value of education. It is in this spirit of investment in the future of the country that public dollars support education.

SUMMARY

School board members are elected because the governance of education is a political matter. This means that the decisions of the school boards allocate resources, and the superintendent and district leaders distribute those resources. When these decisions are made with attention to community engagement and in the context of good governance, they may be difficult, but conflicts may be minimized and the goals of the district, although they may be achieved differently than originally intended, remain the focus of everyone.

The fact that public money supports education in our country is further evidence of the importance of education to our society; we all share in the monetary costs associated with educating our youth. When the public disagrees with the political decisions of the school board, and members of the public do not feel that their views are fairly heard or represented, they have the democratic right to elect someone else, or to become candidates for the school board themselves. In matters of resource allocation, wise school board members are always aware of those areas that are most important to their community.

QUESTIONS

1. How would people in your community explain their support (or lack of support) for public funding of school systems?
2. How does your school board ensure that the community knows the dollars entrusted to it are well stewarded?
3. What are some ways that complaints, and people who complain, may be converted into valuable assets for the school board?

APPLICATION

Consider a difficult financial decision your school board had to make in recent years. What were the steps leading to this decision? How does the decision maintain the vision of the district despite financial challenges? What elements of effective governance could have made this decision more palatable to the parents, employees, and other stakeholders of the community?

FIVE

Democratic Leadership

Board Chair as First Among Equals

The board chair of the school board is the chairperson of the school board. Sometimes people erroneously think that the board chair is the head of the school district. That is the superintendent's role, and one for which he or she is well qualified, trained, and remunerated. The board chair is not senior to the other board members, nor is the chair the boss of other board members; the chairperson is the coordinator of the school board meetings, whose leadership skills are critical to the legacy the board will leave behind.

The role of the board chair is related to the work of the board, not the work of the school district. Everybody wants to be very good at something, and the uniqueness of school board members is that they are going to leave a legacy together. Every member of the school board is elected as an equal at the board table to lead the school district into a bold new future. As explored in this chapter, the board chair role is very important to good governance, but can vary slightly for rural or private school boards.

School board members collectively choose a board chair from among themselves, not someone to be their superior, but someone to act as a chairperson. This is a practical solution because there needs to be a coordinator, a meeting chairperson, and a single voice to communicate with the public, and sometimes one person to communicate between the superintendent and the board membership. This is the role of the board chair.

Chapter 5

RESPONSIBILITIES

As the chairman, the board chair is formally responsible for ensuring that meetings and all board proceedings are in accordance with governing legislation and policies. This is one of the reasons why board chairs do not vote unless there is a tie. Many school boards meet under formal structures, such as Robert's Rules of Order, and the chairperson must be familiar with these rules of assembly to assure appropriate and duly constituted meetings of the school board. Equally important are the community engagement skills of the chair.

Though the chair tends to be the position on the board with the highest public profile, it is a complex role, and one with no authority save that of an elected school board member. He or she must be constantly monitoring and nurturing the interpersonal dynamics and inter-workings of the board toward better governance, while consistently ensuring that the school board is focused on its stated goals. Making decisions alone with the superintendent is actually illegal.

The chair is not the "boss," and must work hard to ensure that, as a leader, he or she understands and represents the will of the board as a collective. Especially in situations where the relationship between the board chair and the superintendent is good, it is easy for the chair to forget that he or she must always represent and confer with the other members of the board in matters requiring the board's approval or consent. Board opinions are registered through public minutes, and so when speaking for the board, it is these views that the board chair must reference.

To govern well, boards need to focus on building solid relationships around the board table, and with students, staff, and community increase their own effectiveness as governing bodies. The popular phrase that "every voice matters" must be an operational reality for the chair of the board. This does not mean that every person has a chance to speak. Some board chairs believe that as long as sound has emerged from each board member's voice box, they have dutifully included "every voice."

The signs of a good chairperson are obvious, but often ignored by school board members, who must be vigilant in reading these indicators. To achieve the important purposes of the school board, the chair must ensure strong and effective working relationships around the table, despite personality differences or preferences. The board and the district are well served when the chair is skilled at collaboration, relationship building, and consensus building. Some highly effective board chairs also acquire formal facilitation, mediation, and negotiation training to maximize the democratic engagement of all members of the board and the district's community.

CONSIDERATIONS

Board members need to be aware of the life stage of the board and the school district, and when they are considering the candidates for chairperson, elect a board chair who is suitable for the times. There are times when a board needs a leader who is particularly skilled at relationships; sometimes it needs one who is able to consistently keep the board focused on its mandate; other times there is a need for a board chair who is willing to lead through difficult and anguishing decisions. Typically, the board chair will bring a personal vision or strength for strong governance to the chairmanship.

Some board chairs have a passion for developing strong working relationships, some seek to improve community engagement, some desire an increased public profile for board members, and some desire accountability measures for their public. Regardless of the vision or style the board chooses for its chair, without doubt the board chair leaves an indelible handprint on the board and on the school district. In this way, the board chair can be the most important factor in board effectiveness or board dysfunction.

According to school board governance experts, the board chair should be the member at the table with the greatest demonstrated understanding of good governance, of meeting procedures, and of the purpose of the school board in its democratic capacity. The chair should hold the respect and trust of his or her colleagues. The board chair does not need to be the friendliest, most popular, or most forceful board member, but must demonstrate governance leadership.

Board chairs need to be very skilled at drawing opinions from members, synthesizing what they hear, and stating the collaborative voice as it develops. The board chair must also be prepared to recognize when it is necessary for a decision to be made, and to draw school board members toward a comfort level so that they may vote with confidence. For those who are the board chairs of their school boards or for those who aspire to be, these skills and qualities are most necessary.

CHOOSING THE BOARD CHAIR

Conventions differ in how the board chair is chosen. Some school boards have a policy guiding the process, which is a wise governance habit that prevents backroom arrangements. Usually, prior to the annual inaugural meeting of the board, board members will discuss together their plans and future goals, availability and interests, and from these mutually agreed upon processes or discussions, will determine who will best serve in which positions on the school board for the following year. Whichever the tradition, and especially if it is policy, the process must be agreed to and followed by all the elected members of the board.

When choosing its chairperson, board members need to be mindful of the type of leadership the board requires at the time, and select a chair who will continue the work of the board toward its stated goals. Sometimes boards need a leader who is particularly good at summary statements after discussions; sometimes they need a leader who is very skilled at leading meetings with the public; sometimes they need someone who can lift the board above personality conflicts and build strong and positive working relationships.

Unfortunately, most chairpersons are chosen because it is "their turn," or because some of the board members want to make "a deal" and others are willing to trade their votes in a crude exercise of politics. Governance literature declares that the strongest board member (ethically and professionally) should lead the board, but school board research suggests that usually the school board chair is chosen for no reason that will reinforce stronger governance or a more effective board.

This, too, weakens the reputation of school boards because the board does not have the type of leader needed at that juncture in the board's development. School board members who cannot choose their own leadership wisely call into serious question their ability and capacity to fairly evaluate the superintendent, or to set proper goals for the district. The choice of chairperson is often a ready indicator of the governance health of the district school board.

The strongest and most effective board chair is the one who has the support of all people at the table. Gaining the support of all board members is an indication of an ability to build consensus and trust. Backroom deals are not unusual between weak and politically motivated board members. However, decisions not arrived at with the consensus of the entire board will serve to weaken both the functioning of the board and the school district it serves.

THE SCHOOL BOARD MEETING AGENDA

One of the primary responsibilities of the board chair is to set the meeting agenda. The school board must do its own work, and the board's opinion of its work is evident in its agenda items. Agenda items are those that the board must discuss because they are governance items. Defining the work of the school board is a critical task and function that should appear in board policy, so that both internal and external parties may understand and evaluate the performance of the board. This clarity also assists confused board members or unelected participants at the board table in understanding why the board meets.

Another critical point for board chairs is to remember that the board must meet for a reason. Often board meetings will not indicate a purpose for the meeting, or any decisions of merit. The board chair must be careful to ensure that when the board is together, it is meeting purposefully.

Designing the Agenda

The vision for the district, the board's goals, and the governance matters defined in policy drive the board's agenda items. The school board agenda should never be filled with administrative matters that the board has clawed back from the superintendent's responsibilities, or that the administration loads onto the agenda to keep the board from productive governance. Many board members complain that they are frustrated because they spend so little time on issues directly related to students, yet it is the board itself, through the chairperson, that sets its own agenda. One of the earliest decisions of every board meeting is the approval of the agenda, so board members can assure that a governance-focused agenda always guide the meetings.

Before voting to approve the meeting agenda, board members can review the governance goals of the proposed agenda, and evaluate whether or not the decisions they are being asked to make are actually the type of decisions made by effective boards. The board meeting agenda is an avenue to excellence and reform for brave board members willing to stand strong for improved governance. A review of agenda items will provide information to the public about the path the board is traveling, and whether or not its stated priorities and goals are evident in its activities.

Another ineffective habit of school boards is to request and include numerous staff reports on their board agendas. If the board is meeting to make decisions, why does it require reports of activities within departments? This invites micromanaging. Though there is often important information to be shared with the board in a public forum, in many staff reports, the board is reacting, ratifying, or appreciating the work of the school district, but not deliberating board issues.

Meetings Are Not to Approve Operational Matters

Boards that require the superintendent to seek board approval for operational decisions defer accountability from the office of the superintendent into the laps of board members themselves, and seriously harm the governance function and the results of the district. Operational matters are the exclusive responsibility of the superintendent, not the board. Boards that make operational decisions are not leading the school district, and are ultimately failing the public who elected them and the people within their schools.

For example, many school boards like to approve the appointment of a school principal, and many board agendas are filled with similar items during May and June. The motives for this are noble, and school board members want to be seen as involved in the important decisions of school leadership, but they do not reflect good governance. Suitable school leadership is the expertise of the superintendent, and a task that should always be delegated to that office through carefully worded governance policies.

The superintendent is capable of choosing his or her own team, and is well educated in these matters. This is another form of evaluation because the superintendent, not the board, is thereby responsible and accountable for the performance of his/her chosen team in the fulfillment of district goals. How can the board hold the superintendent accountable for weak or ineffective personnel if the board itself is on record as putting the final decision in place?

The board must allow the superintendent to staff the schools according to his or her professional expertise, and then determine, through proper channels of evaluation, whether or not it is consistently satisfied with the choices and decisions of the superintendent. If the board finds it is repeatedly dissatisfied with the operational decisions of the superintendent, it must review the suitability of that superintendent for the district.

At no time should the board step in and make operational decisions for which it is neither qualified nor legally authorized. Board members must be careful that such requests are not included on their agendas. General information is acceptable, and may be shared in many creative ways, but not when it detracts from or replaces time required for important board debate.

There are numerous models for effective board agendas, but the primary focus must be on the purpose of the meeting. It is not uncommon for school board members to spend the hours at meetings on matters requiring no strategic direction or approval whatsoever. Board members should keep the mission and goals of the district ever before them, and discuss progress toward those goals. These conversations can include policy review and general oversight. All other matters are ultimately administrative.

Such forward thinking allows the board to plan its meetings across an annual plan that includes policy review and future strategy. The board, however, must itself demand to plan its own meetings, and to have a stated purpose for the meeting. At the end of a school board meeting, the board should have accomplished something and be able to update the public on how the district is doing in achieving the goals set for it.

ENSURING THE MAIN WORK OF THE BOARD

Essentially, the work of the school board sits in four main categories, all of which should guide those items included on the board agenda as board business. It is the chair's responsibility to ensure that the meetings are about these areas of work. The board must set and oversee results; set direction for the district; communicate results to the public; and build trust-based relationships.

Language and goals change with different districts, but basically all boards (including school boards) meet to measure results. Is the work being done? This is an important component of public accountability. Board members should always be able to answer questions from the public regarding the general achievements of the district by clearly defining desired results.

The board also meets to set direction for the district. This is accomplished through a regular cycle of policy review, through regularly revisiting the mission and vision, and by setting the overall direction of the district (e.g., 100 percent graduation rates by year 20XX).

Third, the board must be communicating effectively with the public. Merely establishing a district website is not enough. Not everyone has access to technology, just as not everyone will read a newsletter, or even a newspaper.

Furthermore, the governance role is about communicating the results of the *district* to the public. Some boards think that they need to have pictures of their faces sent home with the students several times a year. While this may facilitate name recognition and even reelection, the board must stand on the record of the district. Honest and effective communication of the school district toward stated goals clarifies for the public that the school board is doing its job well, by making wise decisions regarding senior personnel, establishing governing policies, and setting exciting goals.

In addition, effective communication encourages strong school board candidates. When people are informed and enthusiastic about the work of the school board, they want to participate. While general communication can be challenging in this day and age of diversity and busyness, an effective board agenda communicates the work of the board clearly, and establishes a public track record that everyone, from the federal government to the students, can read and understand.

Finally, the work of the board includes building trusting relationships, both within and outside the school district, with those groups and individuals integral to a strong school system. The board agenda should therefore also include relationship building with different levels of government, interested local groups, and agencies that serve children and youth.

SOCIAL ISSUES

In more recent years, school boards have had to grapple with very difficult issues for which they are perceived to be responsible, but for which they have little training. In these matters, good governance still provides the best answers and responses. These matters include terrorism, guns in schools, vandalism, bullying, racism, alternative sex education, and other social issues emerging in the communities.

A good board chair ensures that the superintendent, and the educators and professionals within the district, have the resources they need to meet challenges for the benefit of all students. When they need support, the chair must assure that the board agenda includes these matters without permitting micromanaging by board members. This is best achieved by a strongly governed board. It is the board chair who guides the meetings and the agendas, and so can best assist the public, the board, and the district in navigating these sometimes very difficult matters.

Many recent publications advise how to achieve effective board meetings. Without exception, the literature insists that all items on a school board agenda should anchor the board's work in governance. Since the work of a school district is both complex and public, designing an agenda that focuses on the work of the board, and not on administrative work, will assist the entire organization to move decidedly and progressively toward the universal goal of better education, and toward the more immediate goals of the local communities represented at the board table.

RESPONDING TO CONFLICT

As in any human organization, there are conflicts on the school board. Research has shown that conflicts can be extremely destructive—especially to a governing board. It is important for good governance that the board table is not encumbered or distracted by poor relationships. It is very important that conflicts not be avoided or ignored when they occur. It is also important that they not be permitted to escalate. Conflicts need to be acknowledged and managed with wisdom. Although respectful relationships ought to be everyone's responsibility, they are especially the responsibility of a good board chair.

One of the key skills for a chairperson is to guide conflict toward productivity, which may sometimes mean involving an expert. There are a number of ways to transform conflict, but some of the simpler and most effective ways have to do with simple knowledge about the nature of conflict and about how people deal with conflict. This section outlines some important tools for board chairs and for board members that can greatly facilitate good relationships and productive board governance.

Since board chairs usually chair most of the meetings, both formal and informal, learning how to recognize and manage conflict is a good skill to have. In fact, it is a good skill for all board members because it is likely that, at some time, every member will serve as the chair. These skills are also useful in conflictual situations with the superintendent, the public, parents, and with labor unions.

Basically, all conflicts are one of two kinds, but both usually manifest as a position. A values conflict involves someone's deeply held beliefs. Values conflicts are usually quite readily recognized, but because moral convictions are involved, they are difficult to resolve. Few school board conflicts are value conflicts. An interest conflict is often harder to identify because the person's real interests may be difficult to recognize or identify. Interest conflicts are usually about matters that are less tangible than what is stated in the position, and are often not publicly revealed.

A simple way to determine which kind of conflict one is encountering is to ask the question "Why?" This may be asked directly of the individuals, but depending on the intensity of the conflict, it may be best to ponder the answer silently. For example, ask questions like, "Why does this person want that?" or "Why does that person need this?" Asking why someone is taking a particular position will reveal underlying interests that are usually not articulated otherwise. Most conflicts can be resolved when the interests of the conflicting parties are understood.

Organizational conflict literature recognizes three general responses to conflict: conflict management, conflict resolution, and conflict transformation. Conflict management skills are really about containing conflict so that a particular goal may be achieved. According to the practices of conflict management, conflict is not really resolved or transformed, but it does not erupt into uncomfortable behaviors either. Conflict management is not good for relationships or for values conflicts, but it is good for achieving organizational goals and timelines.

At the other end of the spectrum, conflict transformation is multifaceted and takes a long time, but in the end, all relationships associated with the conflict will be healed and productive. Conflict transformation is most desirable for conflictual relationships either on the board or between the board and another party or parties, and where interests and values are involved. Conflict transformation is about change, and the processes involved in assuring positive change. Boards that require conflict transformation are best served by engaging in the process under the guidance of a conflict transformation expert.

In the middle of the continuum, and perhaps most familiar to most people, is conflict resolution. Conflict resolution is appropriate for most of the conflicts encountered by the school board, and for those that must be resolved under the guidance of the chair. By definition, conflict resolution processes resolve problems that surface, and can have other benefits like improved relationships. Interest-based conflicts are often resolvable through these processes.

There are a number of skills and techniques required for successful conflict management, resolution, and transformation. Sometimes, the chairperson's approach to conflict may actually escalate conflict in another board member, or there may be issues among board members that simply must be resolved for the board to govern productively. There are books available from the Rowman & Littlefield Education website that can provide some early education. Often conflict resolution skills and techniques are taught in local seminars, and board chairs are particularly encouraged to consider such training.

Conflict Styles at the Board Table

One of the challenges for the board chair is to recognize how people express and respond to conflict, and craft those habits into constructive responses at the board table. In 1972, two researchers named Kenneth Thomas and Ralph Kilmann determined that no two people have the same desires, values, and responses to conflict. In fact, they discerned that people respond to conflict in one of five ways, and they tend to respond habitually, even if the response is inappropriate. These are now commonly recognized as conflict styles or conflict management styles, and are evident in everybody. Recognizing one's own style, and that of another person, really assists in avoiding or transforming conflict.

Essentially, Thomas and Kilmann, and other researchers since, have identified the styles as Avoid, Compete, Collaborate, Accommodate, or Compromise. The manifested style has to do with the relationship between one's own concerns or goals, and the value or the degree of cooperation, one is willing to exercise in the relationship with the other party.

Some authors like to portray these styles as animals, which is a simple and fun way to remember and recognize the styles. According to these typologies, Avoid is depicted as a turtle that withdraws into its shell or an ostrich that buries its head in the same; Compete is a lion or shark that cares nothing for relationship; Accommodate is almost always a teddy bear. The Compromise style is presented as a jellyfish, and Collaborate is an owl.

If someone feels he or she needs to win the argument and does not care about the relationship with the other person after the conflict, that person is most likely to engage in Avoidance or Competitive conflict styles, with Competitive having the highest emphasis on the goal, or on winning. If people are more concerned about the relationship than they are about winning, they will likely manifest Avoidance or Accommodation behaviors. People who use Compromise styles do just that: They compromise, and no one is satisfied. This often results in another conflict.

However, those who value both their goals and the relationship with the other will be Collaborative, and work to resolve the conflict in a way that satisfies both parties.

Expressing Value

Another very important tool for board chairs seeking to minimize the negative effects of interpersonal conflict on the governing work of the school board has to do with how people feel valued. This is very simple, but also very powerful. Dr. Gary Chapman, a psychologist in North Carolina, has written multiple books and has a website about how people can express value to other people, and how they feel valued. In essence, he says that people express value in one of five ways: words of appreciation, acts of service, gifts, quality time, or physical touch.

There is a lot of research and simple human experience that confirms that when people feel valued, they are happier, less likely to initiate conflict, and are more productive. This is an ideal environment for school board relationships.

It is not difficult to determine how people feel valued, because they tend to express it in the way that they feel it. That is, someone who likes to shake hands, hug, and pat others on the back is likely expressing value through physical touch. People who invite others for coffee, meetings, etc., are usually expressing quality time. What is most important is that the expression of value, if misused, can be devastating. For example, when people who feel value through words of affirmation are called names or spoken about dishonestly, they are deeply wounded. For those who express value in gifts, forgetting to acknowledge a birthday can hurt.

Determining how people feel valued, and ensuring that they do, is a positive way to avoid conflicts at the board table and among school board members. This has the additional benefit of affirming the contributions of all people elected and hired to serve the school district organization.

Personalities

The last but often most misunderstood element of interpersonal conflict has to do with the role of personalities. Everyone has a personality, just as everyone has a conflict management style and a personal way of feeling most affirmed. However, in matters of group governance such as the school board, many people, especially elected leaders, dismiss the simple nuances of personality clashes and complements, and blame all conflict on someone's personality. It is rare for the personality to be the source of the conflict, or for a personality to be a problem. In fact, personalities present a great opportunity for crafting a strong board.

A school board, like most elected governing bodies, is comprised of people who must work together productively toward one common goal for at least four years, and when they are elected, voters are not consciously matching and complementing the personality composition that will constitute the voting members of the school board.

Personality typing is a simple conflict management skill for the board chair. Used in conjunction with the identification of conflict styles and of expressions of value, these three simple assessment tools can greatly assist the chairperson. When these conflict management skills are recognized, respected, and exercised by the board chair, they become management tools. In this way, board members feel that they can consistently bring their best to the school board table and not waste vision and energy on unnecessary conflict.

Sometime during the 400s BCE, the Greek physician Hippocrates developed the medical theory that people have essentially one of four personality types, or humors. From this early typography come the modern personality types that often form part of organizational human resource screening processes. Although the theory is not complicated, it is extremely useful and has remained popular across time.

The four personality types, or humors, have acquired many names, and even increased in number over the centuries, but one of the simplest contemporary classifications comes from psychologist Dr. Gary Smalley. In a book cowritten with Norma Smalley and John and Cindy Trent in 1992, *The Treasure Tree* utilizes the images of the Lion, the Beaver, the Otter, and the Golden Retriever (Hippocrates's Choleric, Sanguine, Melancholic, and Phlegmatic), for quick assessments of personality types.

This is a popular tool for seminars and is readily available in a number of forms on the Internet. Although some of the animals are different, board chairs can determine and understand board member dynamics quickly, though on a superficial level, and also recognize how the strengths of the personality types at the table can work together for the goals of the district.

Briefly, the Lion personality is often associated with leadership because it tends to be decisive, opinionated, and comfortable in discussions. However, Lions also tend to think they are right, and make decisions quickly. They are not attentive to detail, so when they make the wrong decision they are not concerned, because correction is simply a matter of making another decision. The real strength of the Lion personality is its capacity for decisiveness.

By contrast, the Beaver personality is very attentive to detail and likes to consider all possibilities before making a decision. Beavers often enjoy working with numbers and making lists; they like to move slowly and systematically through the decision-making process. The real strength of the Beaver personality is thoroughness.

The Otter personality is usually a lot of fun and very outgoing. Otters love to entertain people with wild stories, and are rarely concerned about the accuracy of the details. Otters are usually not concerned with making decisions, and are more concerned with contributing to positive relationships within a group.

Finally, the Golden Retriever personality is friendly, patient, kind, and likes to ensure that any environment they are in is pleasant. They are not overly concerned with decisions, but are very concerned that the process is affirming and peaceful.

Although pure personality types are rare, these generalities are helpful for board chairs, whose primary task is to guide board members through the meeting agenda. Equipped with some tools for understanding that there are two primary types of conflict, for how people manage conflict, for how people feel valued and affirmed (and offended), and some clues toward personality strengths, the board chair can facilitate leadership through stronger relationships with every member of the school board.

CHAIRING THE RURAL SCHOOL BOARD

Although the principles of excellence apply for all board chairs, the realities of the rural school board are somewhat different and unique from the large, urban districts. Most board chairs of rural districts serve much longer terms and are more personally invested in the school district and the community than their urban counterparts. This does not mean there is more sincerity or commitment; only that the situation is different.

Rural school boards have a highly visible role in the community. Often, they are much closer to the originally envisioned school boards of Jefferson's day. The people on the board are key members of the community in terms of farms, business ownership, skills, and general relationships to the school district. Their relationships with the people of the school district and the other stakeholders are also more immediate, webbed, and multilevel than those typically found in urban settings. In many cases, the superintendent and the board chair have known each other and worked together for many years.

Although we live in an era of community engagement, we also live in an era of urbanization and globalization. When political parties that maintain their voter bases in the cities form government, they tend to strengthen urban areas at severe cost to rural areas—for example, by closing rural community healthcare centers, closing schools, and amalgamating school districts across huge geographic areas. Even trade agreements that do not support the local economy can be disastrous for rural school districts and place a particular burden on the school board.

In these ways, the rural board chair is coordinating a number of very difficult, real life circumstances with the governance goals of the district. Paramount to the board chairs of rural school districts are their governance skills. A steady commitment to excellent governance, supported in school board policy and respected by all board members, can assure continued strength among rural school districts for relevant schools and community-engaged boards, regardless of the influences of the external political environment.

CHAIRING THE PRIVATE OR FAITH-BASED SCHOOL BOARD

Private school boards and faith-based school boards are strong boards when they engage in wise governance practices. Often the schools, the district, and the board are structured differently than public school districts and boards. Funding is one of the greatest differences, but funding sources should not deter board members from good governance. Importantly, these factors do not alter the requirement for soundly governed school boards, and they do not alter the requirement for competent board chair leadership.

Also, the composition of the private and faith-based school boards are not usually elected representatives from the public community, although some private or faith-based school board members are selected specifically to fulfill the role of board member because of certain qualities they bring to the board table.

Sometimes, board members are selected for these school boards because of their philanthropic generosity or their personal support of the board chair. Rewarding relationships or generosity is not good governance and can compromise the work of the school or the district in the same way nepotism hurts any organization. The importance of the governance role remains, and the role of the board chair is still to provide governance leadership.

Like public school boards, members of private or faith-based school boards (and often the board chair) are tempted to micromanage school-based matters, and try to behave as "bosses" rather than as governors. This is sometimes evident in the board chair, especially when he or she is the founder of the school, or a senior member of the organization that sponsors the school. Micromanaging is always wrong. The principles of sound school board governance and leadership are fully applicable to private school boards and to faith-based school boards, and the effort to remain focused on governance sits squarely on the board chair.

SUMMARY

The purpose of the school board chairperson is to lead the board. The purpose of the superintendent is to lead the school district. For strong governance to occur consistently at the school board table, the chair must be carefully chosen, and then be attentive to meeting agendas, to making sure meetings are held for a reason and that those reasons are achieved, and to be cognizant of the personalities around the table. With the skills and tools outlined in this chapter, school board chairs contribute significantly to the attainment of the vision and goals of the district, and to the development of a consistently stronger governing board.

Board chairs lead school boards toward the greater goals of education in the district. They are not in charge of the school district, and this applies to private schools and to faith-based schools as well. The chair's role is intimately related to the board's job, not the superintendent's job. The board chair assures the integrity and fulfillment of the board's processes. An effective chairperson leads an effective board, as evidenced by an inspiring mission and vision statement, clearly defined goals, board agendas and minutes that chart progress toward fulfillment of the board's goals, and the board's impressive track record and relationship with the community it represents.

QUESTIONS

1. What criteria would you consider most important in a board chair? Do you see these qualities in your district chairperson?
2. When the board chair is meeting with the superintendent to plan the school board meeting, give three examples of the kinds of governance matters that might appear on the agenda.
3. What is your conflict style, and how do you feel value or affirmation? What are some concrete examples of how these qualities manifest at the school board table?

APPLICATION

Look at the agendas for your school district board meetings for the past year and consider the role of the board chair. Which of the items are governance matters? Does the board chair seem to be running the district, or chairing the school board and its meetings? Look up the mission or vision of your school district, and write a sample agenda that reflects the priorities of the community as you see them.

SIX
Active Democracy

The Collective Strength of School Board Members

School board members provide a key leadership role in the school district; one that only the board can fulfill. School board members are not elected to be superintendents, principals, teachers, or school custodians. They are certainly elected to ensure that competent people are in these roles, but school board members are governors. Exclusively.

Effective board members are mindful of their governance role and resist the temptations to involve themselves in the daily operations of the school system, regardless of the historical behaviors of other board members. Some school board members are tempted to spend time on tangible, non-governance matters and depart from their governance role. This is not good for the district, and it weakens the credibility of the school board.

HOW GREAT SCHOOL BOARDS PROTECT DEMOCRACY

School is where our society comes together for common access to education and where our young learn to live, learn, strive, and grow together. We learn how to link rights with responsibilities, and we acquire much of the skill and knowledge required to live as responsible citizens. Through the common school, the common good is defined and protected. As citizens we have the democratic right and responsibility to choose our educational leaders; we govern the common schools by electing common people as trustees to boards that act on our behalf. The institution of the school board upholds and reflects core democratic values. A well-functioning school board does important work for the future of democracy in America.

Hundreds of thousands of people cannot sit at the board table to guide the direction of the school districts, and so school board members are elected as their representatives. These seven to nine people are democratically elected as individuals to serve as members of a corporate board. They are elected for their individual contributions and unique perspectives, which contribute to the wealth of public trust represented by board governance.

Legislators are valued in our democracy because they are chosen by the citizenry to represent them. In our democracy, federal and state legislators are chosen or removed by the voting populace based upon the acceptability of their track records and their promises. They are also elected or rejected based upon their personal and professional reputations. School board members are elected through majority vote as well, but by a shockingly fewer number of voters (usually well less than 15 percent of the electorate), and rarely based upon these (or any) criteria, according to the research available. Elected school board members in turn determine who will lead each school district, and therefore place the chief executive officer and superintendent.

The superintendent is the employee of the school board corporate. Individual board members are not his or her boss. All decisions from the board are communicated through official records in the public minutes, and the superintendent takes direction from the board corporate in all matters. The district then takes direction from the superintendent. School boards (at least theoretically) delegate all administrative decisions to the Board's only employee—the superintendent, and then hold them accountable for how they apply those decisions within the district.

Superintendents are ultimately responsible for everything that happens within a school district and are responsible for the annual performance evaluation of the district, compared to the goals of the board. In many school districts, for example, the superintendent chooses the leadership of each school, based upon criteria usually established by the board. The superintendent takes the governance requirements of the district to the board, and the board communicates the will of its community to the superintendent. The board makes decisions as mindful representatives of the populations they serve. This is not a discussion of personal preferences, but rather a discussion centered on district goals.

It is a wonderful system when proper government is in action. In reality, of course, this is rarely the case. For example, parents represent about one third of the people represented by the school boards, but even they record that they feel shut out and ignored by their school boards. Ideally, school board members work hard to understand the views of their constituencies, so that they can fairly represent them during school board meetings.

Rooted in democratic values and relationships, school boards are potentially highly influential forces for common good. School boards have opportunities to access educational research through technology and through professional journals like the *American School Board Journal*. Many journals are available online and most university professors present their findings and conclusions in accessible publications.

School boards should be asking questions about the application of valid educational research in their districts because it will help them sort through the many demands on their time. With modern technology, board members also have the potential to question, survey, dialogue, and meet with their constituencies regularly to develop a genuine understanding of their views, values, fears, and concerns regarding educational matters. When school boards and board members find effective methods of communication both to and from their constituencies, they greatly strengthen the positive contributions of the school board to the future of our great nation.

Schooling is the sole institution that provides access to equality of opportunity for all citizens. No other public institution offers the opportunity to acquire skills and democratic values in the manner and for the duration of time that schools do. Children are required, by law, to be engaged in a formal educational process for at least nine years (typically ages seven to sixteen). Education is one of the few vehicles available to our society that offers the opportunity to develop the human potential of each citizen. Furthermore, schools share responsibility with parents for preparing young people for citizenship in a responsible and respectful society. One of the great trusts of the school board is to oversee the development of student potential, through the mindful and strategic governance of the school district.

The role of the school board is not as complicated as modern practice would have us believe. For many of the reasons and evolutions in education already cited, board members are unclear on what makes a good school board, while people not on the school board give school boards little thought. Boards require consensus (decisions everyone can live with), they require initiatives that will improve schooling, and they need to be able to communicate the values of the community to the school district so that the district reflects local values. School boards provide oversight, insight, and foresight. They do not micromanage. The mandate is quite simple.

The purpose of school boards has not changed since their inception. There are so many factors interacting within school districts that board members are often lured out of their roles and lose track of their purpose of ensuring a well-run district. Depending on events in the district and trends in education at the time, board members can be thrust into their new positions with little or no training. There are some steps that help new board members and people interested in school boards to recognize the working purpose of the school board.

The role of the school board member can sometimes frustrate certain persons because it is unlike other elected government officials. The school board member lacks any individual authority. The chairperson is not the "boss" of the board; he or she is the spokesperson and meeting chair. A school board member is not the "boss" of the superintendent or of any other employee of the district. The authority of the school board is in the board corporate. Sometimes this can discourage a passionate board member; many others simply ignore this core feature of school board membership and behave as though they do have individual authority.

This has a disastrous effect on the district, which becomes confused about authority and has its focus pulled away from serving students. All power rests in the board collectively, and it is the responsibility of each and every board member to ensure that the school board is a consistent bastion of collectively strong leadership and governance.

Good governance is not inherent: People do not suddenly acquire the skills of good governance when they are elected to the school board. Governance is a specific role and one that the school board must fulfill. Board members must learn to govern. Good school board governance is not taught anywhere but in the context of board governance, and for most school board members, even then training is optional. When board members understand governance, future candidates for the school board gain a clearer understanding of governance, and the entire district benefits when they are elected.

An excellent book published by Rowman & Littlefield and written by Paul Houston and Doug Eadie, entitled *The Board-Savvy Superintendent*, is a great tool for board members to learn how to clarify their own roles by better understanding the relationship of each board member and the board with the district superintendent.

Although there is certainly media attention for the board member who embarrasses a superintendent, or champions the demands of external interest groups, such conduct does not qualify as effective school board leadership and greatly harms the reputation and the governing of the board. Some school board members erroneously see these and other behaviors as "taking charge" or acting on behalf of their constituents. They are wrong. This is not governance, nor the role to which school board members are elected.

Constituents want good schools. They do not expect their school board members to grandstand by raging into classrooms, publicly humiliating district officials, or meddling in matters for which they are unqualified. Such meddling is actually confusing and embarrassing for staff and students alike, and it is outside the legal mandate of elected board members.

The board must govern responsibly, and allow staff and operational matters to be dealt with through formal processes, not through emotional outbursts. The superintendent is solely responsible to the board for the actions and activities of all employed members of the school district. Board members must maintain the macro perspective of governors, for they are the only officials in the district authorized to fulfill that mandate.

OVERSIGHT FUNCTION

School boards are responsible to *oversee* most of the administration of schools. The actual administration of the school district is the responsibility of the superintendent, who is directly accountable to the board for the tactical management of the school system.

Board oversight includes such matters as the hiring of all school division staff, the maintenance of buildings and property, the provision of learning materials and resources for students, the transportation of students, the development of locally initiated courses and programs, the provision of instructional support services, and the development of policies to govern the operation of the school system.

Though school board members do not actually perform these tasks (and must understand that there are hired employees reporting to the superintendent who do these jobs), they ensure that the right people are in place in the organization through their monitoring of the superintendent.

Good governance depends on the will and ability of board members to understand the distinction between governing and administrating, or managing the school system. The first is the role of the school board; the second is the role and responsibility of the superintendent.

Individual board members can be influential at the school board table, a strength that typically flows from the strength of the community support they have garnered through sincere engagement. They understand that the vote of a majority number of board members will either defeat or triumph a recommendation. Strong board members can influence the district because their contributions are based in the relationships they build and nurture within the community, with both individuals and the public at large, with related organizations, and through professional development.

There are also weak board members who find influence in their willingness to trade the integrity of their office for personal gain by trading votes or negotiating "backroom deals" with other weak board members. This is not the school board member encouraged here, and the popularity of this conduct by school board members is at the core of the criticisms of school boards as irrelevant and self-serving.

The understandings and perspectives that school board members acquire in engaged forums with their constituents allow them to gauge the school district's reputation in the community. These board members also recognize to whom they are accountable, and are transparent regarding the activities of the school district.

GOVERNING WITH PURPOSE

Effective board members increase their general knowledge regarding educational governance while monitoring the level of governing excellence characterizing their board of education. Strong governors recognize and personify the strength of school district governance, and influence the decisions of the board, through honorable channels, toward the continuous improvement of the district.

Across the country, boards are attempting to balance revenue needs, respond to government and public demands, and coordinate systemic priorities in order to make wise decisions for the schools they govern. Parents are increasingly active within their children's schools and, in general, communities are demanding increased accountability, improved communication, and a better understanding of how their money is being used.

Furthermore, school board members are not just accountable to parents—they are elected by and are accountable to the other two-thirds of the general population, which currently does not have children in the school system. School board members represent everybody. Within this evolving context, school board members must maintain their focus. The passion, excitement, and zeal of the initial days on the school board must never be lost, but to make a difference, school board members must direct that energy into effective community engagement for excellence in collective governing.

BOARD DEVELOPMENT AND TRAINING

Board members have historically developed themselves professionally only when they are personally motivated, or when their colleagues recognize the value of board member training, and participate in and encourage professional development. Other individual board members, and entire school boards, feel that no public financial investment should be made to educate the board toward improved governance.

These boards tend to be reputed for their dysfunctional and inadequate leadership. Similarly, there are school boards that use professional development funds for personal travel and entertainment, and this is allowable because their colleagues do not have a policy for accountability to ensure that the expenditure of public money has indeed enriched the board's governance. Each year, thousands of students and thousands of employees are impacted by the decisions made by school board members, and so professional development is a responsible habit of good governance.

Many effective school boards designate portions of their budgets to professional development of each member as standing policy. They take pride in the professionalism of their board members and their high level of effective governance, as proven through their results-oriented progress and reporting. These boards have track records that reflect strong and genuine leadership. Entrusted to guard the public interest in education, school board members are obliged to effectively contribute to their school division as governors, and need to thoroughly understand that capacity. To do less is to weaken public education.

Service as a school board member is rewarding and challenging. It can also be exciting, passionate, and tremendously fulfilling. Educational and fiscal goals demand attention from board members, but the primary need is to stay true to the vision and govern with all the knowledge and integrity they can muster. This picture of the future needs to be the constant focus of school board meetings.

As leaders, school boards must ensure that the world our children will inherit, in accordance with law and local needs and priorities, is at the center of their governance focus, and that high-quality, accessible, accountable education for all students remains the top priority of district activity.

THE HARMFUL LONE RANGER

The composition of school boards is not determined by competency planning, as are other public service boards. They are not planned at all. After each election, the district has the board members who have been selected by the voters. For many people working inside the district, this can be a very real and serious challenge, and a period of lost momentum.

Board members who are carefully trained in governance will be able to work together and serve the district well. Those who are not trained will tend to be lone rangers at the table, seeking to establish a reputation for themselves that is not usually based on a better school district, but rather on their version of board governance.

These board members tend to be deeply involved in district operations, defiant of codes of conduct and reasonable requests for compliance, and become increasingly convinced that their unconventional methods of intimidating district personnel and other board members fulfill the wishes of their constituents. The "lone ranger" board member can both dominate and divide board meetings, so that the work of the board does not focus on continuous educational improvement, but rather on details that the board member can sensationalize and boast about.

Resolving the problems and the harm caused by this type of elected board member is not simple. Training board members properly in excellent governance responsibilities may help to counter the job descriptions they have established for themselves, but often lone rangers are arrogant and refuse to change. Some boards have tried to dissuade these personalities from seeking election by hosting public sessions describing the work of a board member and the role of the school board. Regular meetings with the public often provide a forum where these board members will display their disrespectful styles, and the voters themselves will address their conduct. Sometimes.

In some cases, the stress on board governance and the requirement to support decisions that reflect democratic majority will discourage this type of candidate from seeking office. When they seek office anyway and are successful, board members and superintendents alike will have to work hard to channel the lone ranger's energy and criticisms into productive governance.

School board members have no individual authority, and the district requires a board that will lead together toward a compelling vision of the future. Training board members properly and providing a vision that they, too, can be excited about, will assist the board greatly in developing a governing board on which each member contributes uniquely but constructively.

THE PURPOSE OF BOARD STANDING COMMITTEES

Committee work is an area of school board service in which board members tend to wade into territory where they have no authority and less knowledge. Board standing committees must be used to augment the purposes of the school board, not redo the work of the superintendency and education administration.

School boards have two types of committees: standing committees and special committees. Many boards utilize these two committee types in their regular work, but school boards are a little different and use these committee types for specific purposes.

Each board standing committee is usually chaired by a different board member. The purpose of the board member on these committees is to chair the meetings and then communicate the decisions of the meeting to the board at large. These members get very involved in the discussions and debates of the committees they chair. Like the board chair, however, committee chairpersons are not to participate in discussions. Their role is to make certain that everyone involved has participated satisfactorily in the proceedings.

Often board members are confused about their role on standing committees and feel that they are chairing committees in order to set direction. It is important to remember that the operations of the district are the superintendent's responsibility, and so board members who try to set direction or give directions are acting outside of the authority of their office (all authority is in the board corporate) and are usually violating hiring and reporting contracts.

For most school boards, specific duties (and extra pay) have been assigned to board members who chair standing committees through policy. This decision is the board's to make, but members should be mindful of whether their involvement in district operational decisions drives the board's governance function or shifts the board's attention away from governing. The purpose of the school board does not change, and board members must be diligent in staying true to that purpose when they decide to approve their involvement in district operational committees.

There have been recent recommendations from governance consultants for school boards to consider the use of standing committees to improve the work of the board itself, rather than as a means of involving the board in district operations. School boards need to take charge of their own governance development. Rather than chairing the meetings of district operating departments, board members can each chair a committee that moves the board through continuous improvement.

These committees might include, for example, an Education Research Committee, a Community Engagement Committee, a Professional Development Committee, an Evaluation Committee, a Progress Report Committee, and a Policy Review Committee. The focus of each committee would be governance, not daily operations, and the entire district would be strengthened by the contributions of these committees.

SPECIAL COMMITTEES

Special committees of the board are less common than standing committees, but in many healthy ways reflect the business of good governance. Special committees are established by the board to explore areas the board may wish to introduce to their governance goals.

For example, a school board that wants to learn more about boys and reading might strike a special committee of the board to review current research, consult with specific interest groups, and present a report to the board with its findings. A potential governance directive that could result from such a committee would be a new board goal that would devote specific resources to assure that boys in the district will be reading at a particular level by a particular date.

Special committees allow the board to work at the governance level without confusing the relationships and hierarchy of the district itself.

Special committees allow district employees to demonstrate their expertise in a given area, and to offer sage advice regarding the topic under exploration by the board without experiencing conflicted chains of command.

BOARD MEMBERS IN THE CLASSROOM

Board members like to go into classrooms and schools, and when they are invited, they must respect the authority of the educator leading that class. The classroom is not part of the board hierarchy; board members have no authority in the classroom. Constituents and school personnel usually appreciate their presence, especially at band concerts, plays, etc., but there is a proper way to visit schools that must be rigidly adhered to by board members.

Despite historical behaviors, it is a longstanding tradition of governance that board members do not wander (physically or figuratively) inside the operations of the organization. So it must be with school board members. Invitations to visit schools should be made and accepted through the superintendent. There are many school board members who do not respect this process, and believe that they are fulfilling the wishes of their constituency by "dropping in" at schools and in classrooms whenever they want to. This is, in fact, the job of the superintendent. Hospital board members do not drop in on patients, and university governors do not drop in on university classrooms uninvited.

Most school personnel are delighted to showcase their work to board members, especially those who appreciate the work they are doing, but the proper process is always through the office of the superintendent. Serious work is done in classrooms, and students and teachers need to be allowed to work without unnecessary interruption.

Board members need to respect the office of the superintendent and the responsibilities that have been delegated and/or assigned to him or her through contract and policy. Board members who feel they must visit schools to gain an understanding of the school climate or to gain a sense of the principal's competence must remember that no board member has individual authority, and that proper organizational protocols must be followed.

Good governance requires that board members respect the parameters of their job on the district board, and demonstrate respect toward those people who work inside the district.

NEIGHBORHOOD KNOWLEDGE

School board members are elected from the community, and so bring with them much local knowledge that can be very valuable to the governance of the district. Since much recent leadership literature focuses on the need to serve, to position an organization toward the needs it meets, and to provide resources in response to discerned requirements, the contributions of each member can be vital.

Remember that from their inception, school boards have been intended to govern with knowledge of community needs and recognition of district capacities, many of which are within the experiences of the board members. It is important that school board members are required to learn how to effectively represent the people in their jurisdictions so that the school district reflects the values most important to the communities they serve.

Local values can be quite diverse depending on the community. The definitions of success are as numerous as the districts themselves, which is why they have school board members to determine them. Some communities are very concerned with cost, and an effective school board will understand that, to these communities, this may mean small budgets and maximized dollars—or it may mean more communication so that community members see the value in budget allocations.

Other communities are committed to neighborhood schools and strong learning communities characterized by long-serving teachers, strong parent councils, and community membership and involvement by district staff. Realistically, there are other communities that simply want their students to be literate and to graduate from high school.

Others cherish faith values or specific language preservation, or they have cultural distinctions that they wish to see upheld and supported in their schools. It is the role of the school board to discern which values are most important to its communities, and ensure that these values are protected or upheld in the schools and the school district.

There are key factors for effective school board member development that resonate through board governance literature and the handbooks available to improve school boards. Primary on this list are the sincere desire to ensure better schools, to partner with the citizenry to focus on providing education that reflects the findings of education research, and to address the hopes and dreams of the local community.

Boards that are in constant confrontation with the citizenry and that argue with the policy directions of senior governments have not mastered effective board development. If willing, members of these boards can focus on developing respectful relationships, and use the information that flows to them from those encounters to define the board's vision of its own future, which is different from the future of the school district.

DEFINING THE DISTANCE

While board members are community members, they also have a defined role while sitting officially at the board table. The board meets in a room that is separated from the operations of the school district in a tradition that is highly symbolic of the unique role of the board. The board is not part of the regular functioning of the school district. It usually meets outside of regular organization operating hours. Board meetings are publicly announced.

All of this defines the distance—that is, the figurative and actual distance that separates the world of the board from the work of the district. The actual distance is defined by the job description and task of the board and its membership, as compared to the work of the employees of the district.

It is wise for boards and superintendents to annually review which decisions can only be made by the board, and then, despite the temptation to interfere, adhere rigidly to that agreement. The shorter the list that requires board approval, the better opportunity the superintendent has to demonstrate his or her unique vision and leadership capacities for the district. This also makes superintendent evaluation and accountability a much easier and fairer process, as the board has not clawed back decisions that are, by right, the superintendent's decisions to make.

Some governance literature talks about fences; others refer to sandboxes. Which analogy board members use to remind them of the parameters of their job does not matter. What is critical is that each board member understands that his or her job is not to do the work of the superintendent or of any district employee, and to act upon that knowledge by staying within the confines of governance physically, verbally, and especially when he or she is in the community.

MAKING A DIFFERENCE

Many organizations and consultants train school boards; in training the boards, they work with individual board members. Much of the leadership literature talks about teamwork. This is a critical concept for school systems. In modern school districts, there can be a superintendent's team, a district office team, a technology team, principal's team, etc. Team-building exercises strengthen the capacity of organizational departments, or teams, to provide better service.

But although authority sits in the board corporate, the board is not a team, and its unity in decision-making is not to be based on the strength of board member relationships. Board unity is to be based on a common vision developed through consultation with the public—and through the legislated fact that the authority of the board exists only in the board corporate. At the board table, the board members sit as elected individuals and must carefully make the best decision on the matter at hand. Once they have made a decision, they are united behind the will of the board corporate, recorded for the public in the minutes.

Typically, school boards are told that they need to present a united front to the public and stand unanimously behind board decisions. This is not always good governance. Good board members should be cautiously critical and question recommendations to the board from the administration when appropriate. Those decisions that uphold the vision of the district should potentially produce unanimity. The business of the board is to be united in its common vision, and united in its resolution to strive for the best school system their resources can provide.

The goal is not a united board, and good governance does not require unanimity. Good governance does require collaboration, which means simply that everyone can live with the decision that has been taken, not because majority ruled, but because questions were answered persuasively and members felt confident about the repercussions and outcomes flowing from the decision.

Thus, individual board members should be excellent in the principles of governance, not forced to become good friends with all board members, and especially not good friends with the superintendent, whom they must evaluate annually. Some have suggested it might be better for governance to train members from the same board in isolation so that they can grasp the import of their individual contribution to the governance of the district, and not be distracted from their job by the politics, alliances, and friendships on the board.

INVESTING IN BOARD AND BOARD MEMBER DEVELOPMENT

School boards plan board retreats to strengthen their relationships. These are often very fun, take place at a hotel or retreat center, and paid for by tax dollars. They are necessary. Boards allow for these in their development budgets, or in the slush funds some boards establish for their superintendents, and regard the retreats as a valuable investment in board development—which they can be.

At these retreats, the board is usually working on "team building," and it is a good time. Usually on the recommendation of the superintendent, the board hires an external consultant who works with the board to understand how each thinks and how members can get along with one another. The governance value of board retreats should be communicated and demonstrated to the public.

Although the retreats strengthen relationships between board members, they should not necessitate unanimity at the board table. Visions born of team-building exercises are usually obscure, long-winded, unmotivating, and immeasurable. They are not the shared dream born of consultation, engagement, and accommodation.

According to the fundamentals of democracy, the purpose of electing seven to nine board members is to have individual opinions guarding public trust when evaluating the recommendations to the school board. If there was only the need for one opinion, democracy would not encourage board governance.

It might follow, instead, that board chairs from neighboring districts gather to develop their meeting management and chairing skills, or finance committee members meet to acquire some skills regarding which useful questions to ask during the development and public presentation of the district budget. But board members should not meet to try to develop a united mind. This is contradictory to the purpose of a multi-member board.

It is understandable that boards are pulled into thinking that they need to be a strong and united team. Under the common guidelines of board governance, and under the legislation establishing school boards, the authority of the board rests in its recorded decisions, taken at a duly constituted meeting. Often, boards that abdicate their leadership roles leave the planning of board retreats to the superintendent, who is an expert administrator.

Team building is an administrative tool; it is not a governance tool. Governance requires a multiple-member vote on a request, with a unifying purpose guiding the final decision. Too often, board members think that they need to vote along the same lines as a neighboring board member—their good friend—to assure their opportunity to be the chair.

In fact, board members need to be vigilant and rigorous in understanding the will and desires of their constituency; they need to ensure the board has a vision powerful enough for everyone to champion, and then they need to vote on behalf of their entire citizenry. From the community, the board must forge a vision that each member can support and uphold. The skill of community consultation is one that each member requires, and each member must take that knowledge with him or her to the voting table.

It is not uncommon to watch voting by elected representatives, as it takes place in a public arena, either a school board room or a legislature. It is almost not uncommon to see individual elected officials turning their heads to vote in alliance with someone else. This is wrong. School board members are elected by the public to represent them, not to follow the lead of another politician.

Board members need training, and they need to understand governance. They do not need to be unanimous, but they need to arrive at a common vision through effort, consultation, and discernment among all the education community members. Board members must understand their governance purpose, and find unity in their agreement on the community's vision for education, and through the collaborative processes of governance.

TRAINING THE NEW BOARD MEMBER

In many ways, hope for school board reform is found in new board members. Most new board members do not bring any cultural conformity with them; instead, they bring vibrancy, community connectedness, and some degree of ignorance, which is not a negative contribution.

New board members need to be trained, but they need to be trained in board excellence, not just in district traditions. One of the greatest challenges for new school board members is the conflict between what their governance training tells them should take place and how long-serving board members actually practice their trade.

Without doubt, there is no adequate quick training for a newly elected board member. Time and experience, like knowledge and wisdom, enable new board members to learn to become better public servants. Many boards and school board associations have sought mentoring programs, but since board members are primarily volunteers, these have not been as successful as hoped. New board members are often trained by the superintendent, which is a very expensive process.

Well-governed boards have a handbook and a process established through policy that equips new board members with knowledge about the goals and workings of the district to a level sufficient for most governors. Individual learning about effective governance can be the greatest asset a new board member brings to the school board table. New board members are usually well connected with their communities and represent a perspective that is fresh, informed, and usually more governance-based than the habits of long-serving board members.

Like the work of governance, training new board members is the responsibility of the school board, not the responsibility of the superintendent. The roles are different, and having a board member train a new board member keeps role definition and implementation less confusing.

Most critical to board member training is the public responsibility for sound governing by assuring careful and considered independent thought behind voting choices. Unanimity is not necessary for proper governing. When unanimity is achieved, it should be the result of the proper presentation of a recommendation, thorough answers to provocative and relevant questions, and independent conclusions that this decision is in the best interests of advancing the vision of the district. Board members are not members of a team; they are independently elected governors of a school system that together comprise the legal entity of the school board, united under a common community vision, but never intended to be single-minded.

SUMMARY

American school board members are remarkable in their sincere desire to influence school systems for the benefit of children. Enthusiastic, passionate people eager to lend their strengths to improve the school system are necessary on our school boards. Each board member can bring hopes and desires for change to the table, but it is the collective will that must lead the district. School board members must pause and ponder several aspects of the environment into which they have been elected so they can determine what their personal contributions can be.

Misunderstandings about the work of the school board have resulted in a lack of clarity about the purpose of the school board member and the resultant misunderstanding of the role of the school board. Board members need to be vigilant in assisting their communities to understand their role—once they are clear on what that role is. Many well-meaning but obstinate school board members have damaged the work of the board and the school system it governs by assuming their own ideas of governance are correct, although they have not learned it from any authority.

QUESTIONS

1. What are the qualities of a strong school board member?
2. What specific behaviors must board members refrain from to respectfully reflect their role while in the buildings of the school district?
3. What is the difference between the role of the school board collectively and the role of individual school board members? How does this differ in terms of accountability?

APPLICATION

Look through the board minutes and compare decisions with media sources for matters pertaining to education in your community for the past six months. How do your board members demonstrate their commitment to excellent governance in your district? When you have a problem with something in one of the schools of the district, do members encourage you to follow the channels inside the district, or do they offer to fix the problem?

SEVEN

Ensuring Democracy

The Answerability of School Boards

The public reputation of school boards has much to do with how they regard their answerability to the public. Accountability is a popular word often heard in reference to all levels of government, and certainly a popular word from candidates during school board elections. In fact, though, when people offer accountability, and when others demand accountability, they are usually referring to one of several very distinct concepts, all of which have to do with value. Primarily, they mean answerability. This chapter will explore the various meanings and applications of accountable performance for school boards.

If all that people really meant by accountability in governance was an accounting for dollars spent, in the original sense of the term, accountability would not be an issue. By law, government spending is available to the public upon request for those who are interested. A number of national laws, regulations, and even agencies carefully guide and guard accounting practices across the country.

However, in the service of the public and especially for members of the school board community, the meaning of accountability takes three distinct forms and has more to do with responsiveness and answerability. These are all relationships, and are clearly described in both education administration and public administration literature. Accountability in reference to governance refers to a three-stage process: 1) setting expectations; 2) the pursuit of expected goals; and 3) holding to account for performance. This means that school board accountability is not merely fiscal, and that answerability extends far beyond the approval of a budget.

When school boards are mindful of these three stages in their relationship with the district administration and with the public they serve, they are perceived as, and understood to be, accountable governors. However, there are several areas within these stages in which school boards are vulnerable to accusations of poor accountability.

ACCOUNTABILITY

Accountability in public service is not a new concept, but it is one that has seen much effort toward improvement in recent years, at all levels of government. Although fiscal accountability is highly regulated, accountability for school boards includes the idea that, like other levels of government, members of powerful institutions behave responsibly and respond appropriately to the constituencies they serve. This means citizens demanding accountability are looking less for evidence of responsible spending and more for a sense of value from their representatives. The communication of value is an important consideration for school boards.

Political scientist Paul Thomas has written extensively about accountability, trust, and public service, and the multiple interpretations of these concepts are relevant to school board members. In fact, the elusive meanings of accountability have had negative effects on those who are elected to serve the public. Accountability has become synonymous with responsibility, integrity, control, responsiveness, and transparency—but in fact, most members of the public do not really know what they expect in these terms either. They do want to trust their school boards.

Regardless of which meaning is embraced or intended, accountability is a building block for trust, and trust is established through relationships, otherwise recognized as engagement. In the community-engaged relationships, school boards build the confidence of the general public and members of the educational community. People feel involved and respected by members of the board, which in turn assures a level of confidence and a deep sense that board members are accounting to their communities for the governance of the district. Accountability is a powerful pathway to responsiveness, integrity transparency, and trust.

How Meetings Provide Accountability

What the school board does during formal meetings is the public track record of what it has accomplished, and in this way it provides accountability. Board minutes are public documents because they are intended to reflect the outcomes of important decisions that only the board can make for the organization. In this way, the board minutes are an important form of accountability for what transpires at meetings.

Since the meeting of the school board is an expensive way to conduct business, it needs to be efficient. Most of the district personnel sitting at the table are earning executive salaries; the board members themselves are being paid to be present. Sometimes there are costs associated with meals, heating, parking, and mileage fees for all those included in board meetings. These meetings are very important, but they are funded by public money that is deferred from district operations. As a result, when the board meets, it should be to make decisions that will lead the district forward.

There is a simple way to monitor what the board is doing at its meetings, and that is a review of the official school board minutes. If the board is governing well, these should indicate a consistent and decisive record of achievement and attainment toward specifically stated goals. Meeting for reasons other than to make decisions is common for some boards, but caution should be exercised when this is the norm, because it provides part of the explanation for why school boards are accused of irrelevance.

Sometimes, though, a review of the minutes provides no information to the public, and they are left wondering what it is that the board promised to be accountable for, or how it is that the board is actually leading and governing. Many school boards spend hours approving events that have already taken place or debating and approving matters that are not governance issues. These are indicators of school board members who do not understand their role and do not understand leadership.

Micromanaging

Often board minutes approve an activity that has already taken place, or that is well below the board's governance responsibilities. For example, boards like to approve school trips. Why would a board approve one kindergarten field trip? The district superintendent understands the board's goals for learners, the laws around safety, the capabilities of the professionals in the schools; the principal is aware of the fiscal capacities of his or her school, and has already obtained parental approval on documents approved and established by the board; the teacher is a trained professional who knows best how to teach the curriculum to his or her students. What does a board member know of any of this, and how does granting permission for one kindergarten field trip reflect the governing role of the board? It does not.

The national intention for school boards is to determine the path toward a new future for the children of America; school board meetings are not for decisions that micromanage the activities of the school district. School boards are supposed to meet to make decisions that cannot be made by any other part of the organization.

Few organizations would tolerate a governing board that did not provide goals and proof of attainment for their shareholders through its meetings. It is well documented that many district leaders lament their school boards' tendency to micromanage and to interfere in the daily operations of the district, rather than embracing their significant role as governors.

Few boards would tolerate a superintendent who would deliberately lead the board away from effective governance and embroil beleaguered board members in administrative trivia, keeping the board late into the night, refusing to allow the board to lead, and actively dividing the board to prevent a majority from threatening his or her job. The outraged board members would claim that they were not doing the work they were elected to do, and dismiss the superintendent.

Although such conduct is not characteristic of competent superintendents, this behavior is common to many school boards. There is no one to hold boards like these accountable, except the voting public, who can use the board minutes to assess the productivity and priorities of the board—or the board members themselves. Admittedly, the electoral process is not likely to release such board members, so it is better that they learn how to govern properly, as they had intended when they first ran for office.

Resource Allocation

Since our school system is founded and based on democratic precepts, it has similar problems and challenges to larger democratic systems. Compromise is used by governments, including school boards, in the effort to fairly divide the limited resources of society toward fulfilling people's desire to improve their lot and that of the world community—in the case of the school board, through the processes of education.

Since local school boards want state and federal financial aid, democracy demands that they be held accountable as to the use of the funds. This is perhaps the simplest form of public accountability—how is the money spent? A great reward of leadership is knowing that the job is well done, and boards that exercise the three stages of the accountability process are assured that they are governing well.

In terms of fiscal accountability, most districts employ university-trained professional accountants who are aware of the legislation, regulations, conventions, and procedures of proper accounting. Bureaucratic management facilitates the function of inserting accountability and of utilizing expertise to aid the democratic effort of our school systems. In this way, school boards maintain an external accountability for spending that complies with public policy.

Internal Measures

There is also a need for accountability inside the district. School boards cannot be measured with the same tools that measure student learning, but their performance must be measured. Professional educators are accountable for the progressive learning of students within their realm of responsibility. The board holds the superintendent accountable for what happens in the schools.

School boards need to know that students are attaining reasonable standards of achievement, and benefit from knowing how their schools meet the needs of students compared to those in neighboring jurisdictions. But assessment and measurement of student achievement must not be confused with the public accountability of the school board.

ORGANIZATIONAL ACHIEVEMENT

Some American universities have become proponents against student testing and are discouraging school boards from asking for standards. However, this should not bear on the accountability of the school board for responsible measurement of *organizational* achievement against publicly stated goals, unless the community is asking for student learning measures. The two are different, and it is very important that school board members not be detracted from their purpose by political trends in education practice. School boards are governing bodies; they are not schools.

CONFUSING STUDENT OUTCOMES WITH BOARD PERFORMANCE

There are grave district consequences for school boards that do not differentiate between student assessment for learning, and accountable school board governance. Although school board members may not lose their office, the district and the school experience for learners can be negatively affected by poor members who confuse student learning with board performance.

Consider the opinion of the board member who adamantly carried this thinking to the school board table for nearly twenty years. Complicating this situation was the reluctance and even refusal of some board members to demand accurate evaluation processes for the superintendent, and their assumption that seniority in service years made the board member wise. Of course, the superintendent knew that the reluctance of the school board members to measure the progress of the school district would provide job security for years to come.

This board has recorded, through its legal board minutes, a series of policies under which there is no way this board could hold the superintendent or anyone else in the district accountable for poor performance, and the board members have no evidence to support their campaign promises of "quality education" and "children first."

This school district publicly proclaimed that "weighing the pig doesn't make it grow" in defense of its absurd policies justifying non-measurement of district performance. The school board of this district had confused the role of teachers with the role of governors, and did not establish attainable, measurable performance indicators. This is a failure of accountability and grave misconduct against the population served by this public system.

One of the key tenets of democracy is accountability to the public, and although the school board must have the integrity to provide a track record for their constituents, voters also must be discerning when they vote. It is very important that people outside of school systems understand what their school board does and how the board has pulled the school district forward toward better schools and better opportunities for learners.

Genuine community engagement almost guarantees this kind of understanding. Furthermore, consistent engagement accountability with the community provides a living record that allows the voting public to fairly judge the important contributions made by their school system and school board. The school board is both responsible and accountable to its community to provide information to the general population, and to use measurements to influence the actions of the school district.

MEASURING BOARD PERFORMANCE

Paul Thomas has written extensively about performance measurement, and his scholarship is highly applicable to school boards. Thomas states that social service organizations should give high priority to developing and refining measures of performance. So should school boards. This is not an easy task, and boards must rise to the intellectual challenge of defining performance indicators, and then assuring that the organization, under the leadership of the superintendent, uses the resulting data to find more effective ways to attain the goals identified by the board.

There is a tendency for boards to create indicators that really do not measure anything. For example, what are the actual indicators of "improved morale" or "increased trust?" It is critical that board members carefully design their measurement tools. As the old saying goes, until one defines a destination, one will never know if he or she has arrived. There are many concrete tools for board evaluation on the market, and school board members need to be vigilant in finding or designing one best suited to their local priorities. This is necessary accountability for school boards.

While literature and research continues to debate the subject of student assessment and testing, the accountability of the school board remains an unchanged democratic principle. School boards are elected to govern toward results, but seem to have a dismal record of creating and implementing a relevant set of performance measures and using them as a basis for action to improve board performance. Without clear goals and measurements, there is no accountability for public monies spent, and no assurance that the schools are getting the resources they require. The erosion of accountability is, in part, responsible for the loss of public respect for some school boards.

MISSION STATEMENTS AND ACCOUNTABILITY

Mission statements that describe the ideal future are a ready form of school board accountability for the public and for the organization. Effective mission statements can provide a ready opportunity for all members of the organization to be clear on their daily focus and personally assess whether or not their efforts are pursuing the common goal of the school district. Mission statements cannot contain verbs because they describe how things will be when the board has finished leading. Verbs describe how something will take place; mission statements must describe the future state.

For example, a northern school board stated its mission was to have 100 percent of students reading at grade level by the end of three years into its governance term. Such clarity of mission benefits everyone, and this school district achieved this mission well within the three years allocated, and has since set other aggressive but attained targets for the school system.

Mission statements that lack a clear statement are conducive to avoiding accountability. For example, "fulfilling potential together" does not really hold anyone to anything, but it sounds good. Since there is no way to determine whether or not someone's potential is fulfilled, the organization and the school board can avoid accountability and claim to have achieved their goals. This, of course, is poor leadership, and the board is fooling itself.

But most school board members campaign to make a difference in society and want to provide good schools for America's children. The attention of the school board to a solid mission statement related to the task of teaching children will serve everyone well, and provides the public with a readily recognizable accountability.

Clear goals and mission statements facilitate budgeting, as school administrators and governors alike understand where the bulk of spending must take place. Often the budget can be very confusing, but school board members need to know in broad terms where the district is focusing public dollars. They do not need to debate how many school buses there should be; they do need to determine whether money needs to be spent on getting students to school, and how much of the budget should be allocated there.

A confusing or imprecise mission will lead no one toward the central purpose of the district, and it is usually the students who end up paying the highest price for weak leadership. The guardians of the trust are elected to assure that students are being equipped for the future, not to assure that the school board itself will withstand the tests of time.

Precise mission statements also facilitate policy development. Board members can look at a recommendation before them, consider the mission and goals of their district, and determine whether the board needs to exercise leadership in this area. For example, as stated, boards are often asked to approve events or actions that have taken place days or even weeks earlier. This is foolish. The board must be forward-looking and outwardly focused, voting on those matters that will pull the district forward with adequate resources and guidance.

A clear mission helps boards write comprehensive governance policy and adhere to governance, so that they are free from administrative matters and able to focus on leading. The board minutes should reflect the footprints of the board toward the better future stated in the mission. This is accountable governance.

THE LAW AND ACCOUNTABILITY

There are laws, regulations, and policies pertaining to education and the authority of the school board to which adherence is mandatory. School board members must be familiar with the governing legislation related to the work they do. Modern history has examples of dissolved school boards that were unfamiliar with their legal obligations and parameters, and allowed the school district to contravene the law. Government does hold school board members responsible for their conduct and for their caliber of governance.

In western democracies, there are legal guidelines and purposes for education that provide important information for school board members. In the United States, the federal Department of Education is a Cabinet-level agency established by President Jimmy Carter in 1979, and headed by the US Secretary of Education. (A previous Department of Education was established in 1867, but was demoted to Office status one year later).

Traditionally, education curriculum and standards have been left to local authorities, but recent concerns regarding the will and capacity of school boards and state governments to enforce learning standards has prompted federal intrusions into these previously highly decentralized areas. The main purposes of the federal Department of Education are to formulate federal funding programs for education, and to enforce federal laws pertaining to civil rights and to privacy.

When there is a decline in public confidence toward school boards, initiatives such as *No Child Left Behind* are within the constitutional rights of the federal government. School board members need to remember that they serve at the pleasure of senior levels of government, which are constitutionally responsible for the work of the school board; when the role is not upheld locally, the federal government is not wrong to step in.

In Canada, education is the constitutional responsibility of the provinces and territories; legislatures in turn have delegated that responsibility to local school district boards through education legislation. Similar concerns regarding declining education levels have prompted a number of "school report card" initiatives by think tanks and other concerned citizens, and a plethora of forced district amalgamations and reductions in school boards' powers by provincial governments. There is no federal department of education in Canada.

The school board is a legal entity. The role and responsibilities of the school board and school board members are specific, and are identified within the education laws and regulations of the state. Board members have a governance role. Many new board members believe that they can define their own job and once they are in office, they do precisely that.

Unfortunately, in our democratic structure, there is no authority in any other office in the school district to discipline or remove renegade board members who defy good governance or step well outside their duly constituted role. These behaviors are usually motivated by selfishness and a desire to be seen as a good board member, rather than a desire to build a great school system. Such behaviors reportedly are not uncommon, and they are very destructive to the work of the district as board meetings. Administrative energies are spent answering the demands of these members rather than leading the district forward.

Specific contraventions of the law by school boards have typically fallen within fiscal or personnel areas. Board members ought to be very familiar with privacy laws and with their responsibilities regarding civil rights. Although the superintendent and/or the chief financial officer is responsible for ensuring legal compliance of all activities of the school district, any formal failures to comply are the ultimate responsibility of the elected school board.

There have been boards, with the assistance of bright and zealous superintendents, that have found creative ways to improve the fiscal situations of their school districts that were not illegal, but certainly stretched the parameters of the law (fund-raising, property sales, adult learning centers, private donations are all susceptible in this area). As overseers of district performance, school boards must be careful, as they are ultimately responsible.

School boards exist at the pleasure of the state legislature, and so may be subject to public admonishment or even dissolution if their rash or apparently dishonest deeds or actions are seen to compromise higher levels of government, or if they are seen to be consistently violating public trust. History reflects such interventions. Familiarity with relevant state legislation and regulations will assist board members in making better decisions when asked to support unconventional methods of response to personnel or fiscal challenges.

Finally, school boards are responsible for assuring the corporate competence of the district. While this is one of the responsibilities delegated to and expected of the superintendent, board members need to be mindful of the competencies within the district, and may involve themselves in guiding this aspect of the district through governance policies. For example, the board may establish professional or technical levels of qualification for its employees, including practical experience accounting designations or master's degrees. One of the roles of the superintendent is to serve as chief executive officer, and in this capacity he or she assures that corporate competency and legal compliance are maintained and developed.

BOARD POLICIES

The most immediate legal guidelines in the school district are the policies and bylaws established by the school board. Policies typically fall into one of two general categories: They are administrative policies or they are governance policies. Many school districts are moving toward a dual set of policy manuals to assist in the task of focusing on governance and avoiding administrative interference. These boards have delegated the responsibility of administrative decisions officially to the superintendent, who develops all administrative policy.

The board is free, then, to be familiar with and focus upon the governance purposes of board policies, and is also able to place responsibility for unacceptable administrative behavior completely in the office of the superintendent. For example, many board members have stated that when they pass hundreds of administrative policies, they feel responsible for them. This sense of responsibility invites questions and requests for information on operational matters that would not be in their purview if they had not been the ones to approve the policy.

In the end, it is the school board, as the legal entity, that is ultimately held responsible and accountable for activities of the school district. For this reason, individual board members must familiarize themselves with all legal documents pertaining to their elected responsibilities.

ETHICS, TRUST, AND THE SCHOOL BOARD

There is a growing body of literature merging the disciplines of public service and ethics and trust, which have real implications for modern school board members. In our North American context, we are moving away from what were once common objective social standards of ethical behavior, and defining ethics in increasingly subjective terms. With the emergence of the rights dialogue, responsibilities are also changing, and so defining a universal ethical code for the school district is becoming more and more often a responsibility of the board.

School board members, as part-time governors, bring their own sets of personal ethics to the table. Interestingly, this is a character quality that is rarely, if ever, mentioned on campaign literature. It is assumed that the elected leaders of our school districts will be ethical and trustworthy.

What does it mean to expect ethical behavior from the board? What does it mean to trust? First and foremost, it means that the community senses and has evidence that the board is accountable to them. School boards must do what they are elected and expected to do. We expect they will be honest and fair, just and kind. These are some of the basic premises of democracy, and so we can expect these characteristics from our elected officials. History has not always supported this trust, though, and sometimes ethical behavior is easier to describe than identify.

We expect board members to do what they say they will do. When they tell us they are concerned about students, teachers, and prudent spending, we find ourselves questioning their ethical standards when their conduct does not match our expectations. For board members, meeting public expectations for ethical conduct is not as easy as it sounds, nor is it simplistic.

For example, boards must perform the job that only they can perform in the district, and must be aggressive about ethical leadership. Most of the time, this means making a firm decision to consistently keep out of the jobs of hired personnel in the district, and to ensure that the district is run well. While it is tempting to become involved in daily matters, board members must be vigilant in their governance role and avoid involvement in district, school, and classroom administration.

School boards are elected to govern, not run the school district. Superintendents are executives who expect their boards to do their job and provide leadership, so that superintendents can do what they ahev been educated and trained to do: administer the school district toward fulfillment of the vision through achieving the goals of the board. Often, though, boards will spend hours debating a decision that has already been rightfully made by the superintendent, or determining the outcome of an event or circumstance that is not theirs to determine. This is an ethical violation.

An Example

Consider the following example of a genuine ethical dilemma for a governing board. There once was a school board whose members were highly committed to their community and to an honorable working relationship with their superintendent. They invested many dollars each year developing their governance capacities, fairly and objectively evaluating their superintendent, and establishing goals and performance measurements that would help them recognize the consistent and annual progress of their school district. By most measures, this district was fulfilling its commitment to excellence.

But at the same time, the board maintained a policy that authorized different individuals on the board, by name in board policy (although many of the names were no longer elected board members), to determine, as individuals, whether or not a school would be closed due to inclement weather. According to policy, one board member would contact the principal of the local school by telephone, who would notify his or her staff, and then the transportation personnel, that the school in their ward was to be closed.

At some time during the course of the day, quite literally through the public grapevine, the superintendent would learn that a school had experienced what is known as a "snow day." Board members vehemently defended this policy, insisting that this behavior had a long history in the geographically dispersed district, and that it demonstrated to the communities that their elected board members were concerned about the safety of the children. They were simply wrong. This is a prime example of unethical board behavior.

The board members must *never* forget that they have *no authority as individuals*. All authority rests in the board corporate. For the implementation of the snow day policy described above to be in any way legal, there needed to be a special meeting of the board, called by the chairperson, with the consent of *all* elected members, according to the state legislation of this jurisdiction. This would require forty-eight hours public notice. Then the entire board would have to be convened, a recommendation presented and voted upon, then recorded in board minutes as an official decision of the board. Of course, none of this could take place in the immediacy of a snowstorm. But there are other reasons that explain why this policy was unethical.

The superintendent is the board's greatest resource, and the board described here certainly concurred with this evaluation. The conduct of the board described above is extremely discourteous and disrespectful to the superintendent, who, according to the policies of this same school district, is the *sole* employee of the board. The behavior of the board members was outside legislative authority.

In effect, the board had contradictory policies that it needed to update. It is *exclusively* through the office of the superintendent that the board has contact with the administration of the district, and this fact should have made the snow day policy obsolete. But without regular monitoring and evaluation of the policy manual, the board did not know of these contradictions. Board members have no authorization to give direct orders to a principal or to the transportation supervisor or to the bus driver.

The one employee the board is required to communicate with, the superintendent, was not included anywhere in this well-established tradition. Board members who feel they are acting in the public interest by directing district employees confuse employees (many of whom are unionized within a specific chain of command), erode the credibility of the superintendent, and put themselves in a completely illegal situation.

Ultimately, although members were motivated by a sincere desire to be a good school board, this board recognized that its behavior was illegal, unethical, and unnecessary, and after much heated debate determined that it would leave the decisions surrounding poor weather conditions exclusively to the superintendent.

Some days, a board member will call the superintendent by cell phone to inform the office of poor weather. Usually, by then, the principal has contacted his or her direct supervisor, and the decision has been made, teachers have been notified, and the administrative structure of the district has notified the transportation supervisor, who knows which personnel to contact in that department. The superintendent has delegated other responsibilities, such as notifying the radio stations of the school closure, to the capable staff of the district. The board now follows ethical conduct in this matter, and there is no confusion.

WHEN THE SUPERINTENDENT IS COMPROMISED BY THE BOARD'S BEHAVIOR

Superintendents are hired, evaluated, retained, treasured, and sometimes released by the board. An unethical board is a very difficult professional challenge for a senior employee, who must advise and admonish those who are his or her collective employer. This produces a strange reversal of roles, as the superintendent is required to employ the ethical and professional leadership role that is the responsibility of the elected board *against* the elected board, for the sake of the school district.

In some cases, though, the board does not appreciate this responsible conduct, and insists on exerting both power and authority inappropriately, often individually. This is an extreme violation of ethics and trust on several levels, and only harms the work of the board and the district.

The example of unethical behavior below comes from a board with district-oriented intentions from some, but not all, board members. Like the board described above, this board had very good schools, with well-respected principals, hard-working teachers, and students who achieved well on tests of general learning standards. Annual evaluations of the board and of the superintendent indicated a consistent movement toward improved learning.

The greatest challenge in this school district, according to superintendent groups, the public, school board associations, and other education stakeholders, is the board itself. There are several dominant personalities on the board who seem committed to unethical behavior—all in the name of excellent public service!

It is not unusual for individual members of this board to march into classrooms uninvited, rage at teachers, threaten the jobs of principals, and then bully the superintendent at the board table, all the while insisting that they are doing the work they were elected to do. Such outrageous, illegal, and unethical behavior spills into other governance areas.

In this example, the board was requested by the community to change the name of a school. After very thorough and extensive consultations with the public, the staff, and the community directly involved, the board had documentation that between 80 percent and 90 percent of the community supported the proposed name change. There was much media publicity. At the following board meeting, the board voted against the change on the grounds that it did not have a policy for the process of school name changes.

The community was outraged, and due to the highly publicized media coverage of public opinions, five of the nine board members lost their seats in the following general election. In this situation, the board tried to err on the side of caution, but was instead seen as unethical and unreliable. Within days of the board's non-decision, the superintendent announced his retirement.

Unethical conduct seriously erodes the credibility of all school boards. The damage is far more extensive than board members might realize. Reputations are very, very important in public service in particular—especially for leaders. Since board members are elected to a part-time office, they are often not aware of the debilitating effects their unethical conduct can have on the organization. Unethical board behavior, and board member behavior, filters quickly through the school district, and can distract the employees of the district from their central focus—helping students learn.

Unethical behavior also distracts superintendents from their important work, as they focus their energy on coping with the board. For example, the superintendent, or other highly placed administrators, can spend many hours visiting schools in the wake of interfering board members, encouraging principals and teachers and mitigating the negativity of the individual board member, who under no circumstances is authorized to individually visit a school, issue orders, or demand particular conduct.

Without the written authority of the board appearing in board minutes, this board member is outside the law, and well outside the ethical responsibilities to the public that elected him or her.

ETHICAL CONDUCT AS A BOARD MEMBER

Ethical board members are a great asset, and strengthen the entire board. They uphold the spirit of public trust, stay out of the superintendent's job, and work with other board members to constantly improve the governance capacities of the board. An increasing number of school boards have tried to establish common codes of ethics in an attempt to ward off unethical conduct. Part of the very real problem with this exercise is, again, the varied interpretations of "ethical."

In extreme cases, dysfunctional boards have used their codes inappropriately to control or bully other board members. In contrast, those boards that focus their time and energy on wise governance, building trusting and authentic relationships with their communities, ensuring they have the right superintendent, and leading the district through governance decisions, do not typically struggle with ethical misconduct and do not require a policy to inform them of such.

Ethics and trust are another example of local values and belief systems, and each are usually clearly understood by the community the school board serves. By relying on an engaged community to explain and define these concepts, school boards can keep themselves free from accusations of unethical and distrustful conduct and, most importantly, from alienating their community and creating unnecessary conflict.

Essentially, the work of the school board falls into four main categories, all of which should guide those items included on the board agenda as board business:

The board must set and oversee results. Language and goals change with different districts, but basically all boards (including school boards) meet to measure results. Is the work being done? This is an important component of public accountability. Board members should always be able to answer questions from the public regarding the general achievements of the district by clearly defining desired results.

The board meets to set direction for the district. This is accomplished through a regular cycle of policy review, through regularly revisiting the mission and vision, and setting the overall direction of the district (for example, 100 percent graduation rates by year 2020).

The board must be communicating effectively with the public. Merely establishing a district website is not enough. Not everyone has access to technology, just as not everyone reads a newsletter or even a newspaper. Furthermore, the governance role is about communicating the results of the *district* to the public. Some boards think they need to have pictures of their faces sent home with the students several times a year. While this may facilitate name recognition and even reelection, the board must stand on the record of the district.

Honest and effective communication by the school district on progress toward stated goals clarifies for the public that the school board is doing its job well, making wise decisions regarding senior personnel, establishing governing policies, and setting exciting goals. Furthermore, effective communication encourages strong school board candidates. When people are informed and enthusiastic about the work of the school board, they want to participate. While general communication can be challenging in this day and age of diversity and busyness, an effective board agenda communicates the work of the board clearly and establishes a public track record that everyone, from the federal government to the students, can read and understand.

Finally, *the board builds trusting relationships both within and outside the school district* with those groups and individuals integral to a strong school system. The board agenda should therefore also include relationship building with different levels of government, interested local groups, and agencies that serve children and youth.

There have been many recent publications advising how to achieve effective board meetings. Without exception, the literature insists that all items on a school board agenda should anchor the board's work in governance. Since the work of a school district is both complex and public, designing an agenda that focuses on the work of the board, and not on administrative work, will assist the entire organization in moving decidedly and progressively toward the universal goal of better education, and toward the more immediate goals of the local communities represented at the board table.

SUMMARY

School boards are accountable to the public and to their school districts in many ways. In matters of fiscal accountability, the federal government maintains rigorous legislation and regulation to ensure the school districts and other public bodies are in compliance. These matters are attended to by university-educated accountants employed by the district. But accountability is not always used this way by governments and members of the public who are scrutinizing or questioning the work of a school board. Accountability is also answerability, reliability, trust, transparency, responsiveness, and control.

Providing evidence of school board achievements is mandatory for school boards in order to show themselves as excellent to watching eyes. Accountability in reference to governance refers to a three-stage process: 1) setting expectations; 2) pursuit expected goals; and 3) holding to account for performance. This is an era of opportunity, and school board members can demonstrate their importance as vital and relevant leaders by establishing a track record of proven performance through the many windows of accountability built into the governance system. And the public will then know that board members are, indeed, governing the district well!

QUESTIONS

1. What are the ways that school boards are accountable to the public? What structures do they use to do this? What are the synonyms for accountability, and how are these provided by the school board?
2. Develop working definitions of ethics and trust for your school board, according to the values and beliefs in your community.
3. Choose a small number of school board meetings that have occurred this past year. Examine the agenda and the minutes. According to these few documents, what is it that your school board has done to definitively achieve its vision?

APPLICATION

Think about the responsibilities and expectations for school boards. Write an accountability policy for your school board (not district) that begins, "In our district, the school board is answerable to the public for . . ." In your policy, give consideration to the message in the language you would use, and how the board, and school board members, would be measured.

EIGHT

Encouraging Democracy

Carefully Designed Culture

When people use adjectives while talking about the atmosphere or environment of the school district, they are referring to its culture. They may say it is welcoming or intimidating or fearful or empowering. Culture has been described as those things we all know we all know. This is a good descriptor for school board and school district culture. This chapter explores the influence of organizational structure and culture on the work of the school district, and encourages school board members to be very aware of the culture within their district.

We also all know what a good culture is; we know when culture is painful or discouraging and prevents democratic participation from board members and from community members. There is a lot that boards can do to protect their district from dysfunctional cultures.

For example, school boards working within the political confines of hierarchical bureaucratic structures find their work to be typically restricted and controlled, which indicates that they have a dysfunctional school district culture. Usually, unhappy district cultures are the result of the superintendent's leadership; if the district is happy but the school board culture is unhappy, it is the result of the board chair's leadership.

But a positive and encouraging culture can be designed regardless, and this is one of the key contributions of the school board! It is within the authority of the board to protect the work of the organization from its structure. That is, school district structures, including the organization chart, are recommended to the board for approval. Many board members believe that any board involvement in the structure of the school district is micromanaging, because they have been told this by people who do not know. It is not micromanaging, and it is a serious responsibility of the board. Although the superintendent must structure the district according to what is needed for education, the board can provide careful oversight and perspective.

For example, some large bureaucracies do not share any of the cultural qualities associated with positive learning, and in times of fiscal restraint and cuts to education funding, people are discouraged or afraid for their jobs. There is fear, which in turn breeds divisiveness, competition, and secrecy—and steady employee turnover. Such an organization can bear down and choke out the responsiveness and creativity required in educators to teach the young.

The school board must also learn to recognize counterproductive control, which may become more prevalent with the increasing size of bureaucracy in the modern school system. The board should be aware of this inherent danger, and avoid or correct the problem by giving careful attention to the organizational structure in each decision it makes, and it must be attentive to the behaviors and recommendations of the employee it has hired to make the central decisions within the school district—the superintendent/CEO.

School systems were established to serve young learners, and school boards that allow the district to focus on other matters quickly have dysfunctional and inwardly focused organizations to govern. Through policy and community engaged practices, the board must point the school system outward, toward the people it is serving, and resist the temptation to focus inward. Deliberately establishing structures that encourage community engagement cause this to happen naturally, through the daily operations of the district. An organization built to engage will not easily become self-serving.

Another problem that creates a negative culture is that many modern school districts demand that teacher and school leader creativity take place within a structure of permissions and control. Instead of encouraging and empowering, it wears people out. The school district becomes characterized by discouraged teachers, early retirements, transfers to neighboring school districts, and high numbers of teachers on stress leaves.

This is the greatest challenge of school systems: They may appear accountable in terms of rules and on paper, but in fact they may be stifling the very life needed to meet their fundamental purpose—to respond to the learning needs of each student in the system—by the structure and policies approved at board meetings.

The signs are obvious when board members are alert, but often ignored by school board members who are not thinking forward. Board members must be vigilant in reading these indicators, because structural reform is usually subtle and incremental. Although many people think big school systems are impersonal and that bureaucracy chokes out creativity, in fact, the structure of school systems provides an opportunity for great governance.

School districts need to foster passion and creativity, and this cannot take place within a rigid structure of permissions and bureaucratic authorities. It is the responsibility of the board to ensure that it is engaged with its communities in meaningful ways, so that its members can assure themselves and their critics that they have established a school district that is conducive to maximized teaching and learning at every level. It is also the responsibility of the board, through policy and monitoring, to ensure that the superintendent is equipping and empowering people as the board leads.

CULTURE AND VISION

A school district must be structured around the district's culture and purpose, though it is tempting to focus on an organizational chart instead. Policies, programs, and procedures are responses to locally defined and determined values, beliefs, and resources. Often, the local community is defined or restricted from expanding because of the policies and programs of the school district.

To mindfully structure the district around the community is a huge leap forward for school boards, which have lived within and carefully maintained the bureaucratic structures of education for decades. Without the full leverage of the many abilities and talents within the modern school system, student needs cannot be satisfactorily met. School boards must pay careful attention to the culture of the school district, and be willing to tackle entrenched policies so that the district reflects and enables its purposes rather than choking out the fire that board members are elected to ignite.

Boards may blindly tolerate something that is not working anymore by merely assuming that the best interests of an organization will also fulfill its community goals. School boards can lose sight of the purpose for which they exist, and reinforce an administrative structure that cannot allow professional educators to do what needs to be done. It seems that people outside of the boardroom, and even outside the industry of education, recognize this, but board members working closely with the district do not.

Often, newly elected members are aware that the school district has not succeeded in achieving its stated purposes, but their voices are dismissed by longer-serving fellow board members. School boards are elected positions of leadership, and governments across the continent are reluctant to abolish them completely. This means that the boards have the opportunity to provide the vital and mindful leadership our school systems need today, instead of maintaining archaic and stifling structures and styles through inattentive governance.

If we fail to build school systems with a clear vision of the future, we will not have a future ourselves. This mandates that the needs of the learner, not the existing structures of the school district, be the focal point of governors. School systems must be constructed around the student; the students must not be filtered into a self-perpetuating structure.

Schools must be culturally relevant, student focused, and forward oriented. School board members are elected to set the vision and lead the school district toward the future with courage. This is the challenge in modern education—to boldly articulate a realistic yet inspirational future while standing against opposition, conflict, and even the tyranny of administrivia, to make sure that future happens.

Sometimes a school board is reluctant to admit that its district is simply not making a difference. Astute board members must look past the desire to only celebrate and self-congratulate, and ask whether the school district is meeting its goals, regardless of what appear to be signs of success. There will be graduates every year, there will be new teachers every year, there will even be increased enrollments or building additions. But these signs of growth do not mean that the school district is healthy, or that it is effectively developing the human potential within its jurisdiction.

As representatives of the public and guardians of their trust, school board members need to be alert to the internal culture of the district. It is difficult for board members to stand back to see what is really happening and to exercise appropriate governance. It is a well-established fact that leadership shortcomings are typically felt more by those inside the organization than by those at senior levels, such as the board, and so board members have to be careful to be balanced in their attention to indicators of district health.

LOCAL DEFINITION

Ultimately and ideally, great school systems are defined locally. Through extensive consultation and an ongoing relationship with their communities, school board members work with all those interested in education to pursue a commonly defined vision. The vision is not imposed; it leads people. School boards cannot be mere caretakers of the tremendous national resource emerging through the processes of education.

Board members must be leaders, portraying discipline and perseverance in the pursuit of outstanding school systems. Such discipline and perseverance is a direct response to a contagious and common vision. People hone their energy toward fulfillment of that vision.

It takes discipline on the part of each board member to not be drawn toward administrative meddling instead of leadership through governance, and to establish a vision that produces focused and deliberate activity relevant to the community they serve. America needs school board members who will discipline themselves to provide that which only school boards can offer to school systems.

DESIGNING THE CULTURE

Cultures are an integral part of an organization, and they exist whether they are designed with care and foresight or develop through default. Modern organizational literature suggests that it can take approximately eight to ten years to develop a positive, nurturing, and exciting organizational culture, but less than two years to twist a great culture to a controlling or corrupt culture. The responsibility for avoiding such developments is principally, of course, that of the school board, and guarding the trust of the public and the employees of the district, for the sake of the students especially, ought to be of paramount importance to board members.

The culture of the school district can be a source of great mystery and frustration to school board members, who often blur their contributions to the district as somewhere between "boss" and employee status. Typically, people not sitting at the board table are more in tune with the corporate culture of the district than board members are, meaning that they can be a great source of engagement when the board needs to monitor the actual climate of the district culture.

Since the board is responsible for building a culture conducive to successful learning communities, it is imperative that board members and the board itself adopt a methodology that will allow understanding of the authentic culture of the district, not just the one intended by the mission statement or vision, or the culture that senior administrators describe. This is one of the core contributions of meaningful, ongoing community engagement.

Understanding the culture of the organization can help board members understand why initiatives fail, why change does not happen, or why projects do not get off the ground. It can also offer real explanations for staff turnover, student attrition, and disgruntled parents. Most often, these answers may be found through an ongoing and engaged relationship with the multiple communities of the district.

MONITORING THE CULTURE

Corporate cultures in school districts develop as a direct result of the superintendent's leadership style. Board members must use their influence and communication skills to fully understand whether the district culture is a fair representation of community values. Through appropriate feedback mechanisms, the board is able to exercise its governance function in part through assessment of the district culture.

Sometimes boards believe that creating mission statements or policies that contain words like "empowering," "trusting," "nurturing," or even "exciting" will assure that the culture within the district will reflect these qualities. This is not so. Words are not enough. Boards require mechanisms to monitor that the district is progressing toward its objectives, and must be able to identify the causes or risk factors inhibiting achievement of those goals. The culture is a strong indicator.

Culture can be nurturing or stifling, and either is within the control of the school board. School board members are obligated to provide relevant school systems, but for a number of reasons do not. Some board members think that whatever is recommended to them, or whatever is happening in the school district, is just the way things have to be. This is not leadership.

Some school board members cannot actively envision and plan for the future because they use unreliable measurement tools, which leads to the assumption that what is happening in the school district works. Sometimes board members passively accept what administrative or educational experts propose, and accept the status quo. Some feel intimidated, while others talk, debate, and write new mission statements that miss the mark for an invigorating future.

One of the reasons we elect a board to represent us is so that it will fight for a great school system for our children. This can mean questioning a recommendation, or revisiting a strategy that has been at work in the school district. It can even mean resisting the opinions and unexcited minds of fellow school board members. Unfortunately, making a fuss, writing fine slogans, and passing many comprehensive policies cannot substitute for effective leadership.

When a board has a clear vision of where it envisions the district going, most administrators will utilize all their expertise to achieve those goals, and a vibrant culture results. The future cannot be held hostage by lazy minds, burned out and/or ineffective school board members or ineffective superintendents. This has been the fate of many school boards, but it is time to change. The board can decide that the school district will be great, and undertake the necessary steps to make that vision a reality.

If the board does not lead in this critical function, and aggressively define the path for the school district, its demise will be justified. The board can shape the culture of its organization by designing district structure around the culture, instead of allowing the structure to determine the culture.

CEOs are authorized to change structures on behalf of the board (which they tend to do through expansion), but it is the governing board that can decidedly establish a culture of innovation and learning through the decisions board members make every time they meet. Deliberate attention to culture evidences strong school board leadership.

THE DIFFICULT DECISIONS

While discussions and assertions of pressing community values into schools are found in most books and articles about the role of the school board, an example based in real life can illustrate how culture can influence whether this works or fails in the exercise of school board governance.

A very real dilemma that faces many school systems is insufficient funding. A ready solution to expensive budgets is to close schools. This is usually a very painful situation, and board members often find themselves in hostile situations with the very people they have been elected to represent.

In this scenario, imagine that citizens greatly value neighborhood schools, and although enrollment is low for the capacity of the building, enrollment in this school has been constant for many years. Citizens, parents, and students value this school and recognize its integral role in their community.

Using the knowledge we have gained so far about the role of the school board, one would assume that the school board would be in conflict with the superintendent and administration, insisting that the community values this school greatly, and so there must be an alternative way to save the dollars the superintendent proposes to save by closing the school.

Sadly for most school communities, the antagonism would be between the board and the public. Petitions and requests by community members to the board would be ignored as the board stridently defended its own position. In this scenario, the board feeds the erroneous notion that school is a cost, not an investment. For a board with the authority to impose local tax levies, the closure of this school should never have been a community-dividing issue, and the board, elected to press local values into the school system, has turned a deaf ear to the values of the community.

In those rare times when the board absolutely must make a very difficult decision, it must work carefully with its communities until most stakeholders understand and can live with the final decision. The board's allegiance is to the community it represents, not to defend unreasonable preferences or comply with demands to save money in ways that violate community values.

There are other times when, for some reason, the board must make decisions that are not in keeping with the views of the community. These are difficult, yet at the same time it is critical that the board embrace its primary role to liaise with and engage the community until a consensus can be reached regarding the decision. At these times, the strength of the community/school board relationship is extremely important.

A consensual decision is not necessarily a full embrace of a decision, but it is strategic for implementation that everyone can live with the decision. However, a board that has earned the trust of its constituency can work in collaboration with the public and the superintendent, and together the troubled times can be addressed, solutions worked out together, and the issue can be resolved with the good reputation of the board and superintendent intact. This is very important, and one of the hallmarks of consensus building and community trust, and another area in which school boards may set an example for other levels of government.

PRACTICAL STEPS TO BUILDING POSITIVE BOARD CULTURE

There are practical steps school boards can take to build a board culture that demonstrates respect for the values of its community, and that draws feedback from the constituency to strengthen the relationships between the schools, the school district, the board, and the citizenry.

One of the first areas board members must examine when evaluating the political climate around them is whether or not the board communicates an attractive message. No matter where the board serves across this great country, its message usually needs to be one of excellence. Few people want to support a board or a district that is just doing its best, or hoping to be better than last year. They also do not want to have to stop and figure out what it is the board is trying to say.

Overall, the message of schools is a simple one: They teach kids how to learn. When board members are truly excited about the message they want to convey through the direction of the district, it usually is an exciting message, and one that the community will be excited about too.

Board members who are genuinely concerned and humble are attractive to constituents. Most people can see right through "edu-jargon," "board-babble," and insincerity. Board members who seek to authentically listen to the concerns, visions, and hopes of their constituents usually succeed in creating a board culture that draws valuable communication from the community.

On the other side of this, boards that draw angry parents, angry crowds, and public scorn are usually comprised of board members who have failed to create a sincerely welcoming culture. Words may deceive some people for a while, but attitudes are always true. A warm and welcoming mission statement becomes another source of fury toward the board when board members are insincere, or are not ensuring that the superintendent is aligning the district with its mission.

The mission of the district is critical for many reasons, but as a tool to leverage public opinion, it must guide the contributions of the public in the same way that it must guide and focus the work of the district. When the public has a clear sense of the direction of the district, people are able to direct their comments and suggestions usefully. When this is coupled with a sincere desire to listen and acquire input from constituents, the board is well on its way to building a strong communal relationship.

For those honest board members who recognize that they need to build a respectful and effective relationship with their constituency, it is not too late to start. Much can be accomplished in a four-year term. In many ways, four years is the term of excellence in the western world: after four years, we evaluate our politicians, after four years we have our Olympic athletes defend their titles; we spend four years in high school, and four years acquiring a university degree. School boards can revolutionize their jurisdiction and redeem their reputation in a four-year term if it is necessary, and if they are willing.

An excellent tool for leveraging the opinions of the public is to present a clear picture of the school district as the board sees it—for example, a large banner stating simply, "The school district we see is . . ." and signed by the board members offers a public and compelling vision for anyone who sees it. Points should be made briefly, accurately, and concisely. They should not constitute verbose statements that encompass each and every value of every world political system, world religion, and politically correct definition of the learner. They should not contain words that are difficult to operationalize.

For example, words and phrases like "safe," "potential," "positive learning environment," and even "excellent" really do not mean very much when the public is trying to understand what it is that their school board sees for the district. Words like "every classroom equipped with a book for every student," or "the best jazz band in the state," or "teachers with the right resources to challenge each student," communicate excitement, purpose, and a precise direction. People will respond to statements like these, and the board can know it is making decisions based on the values of its community.

Some boards have also found that inviting groups to meet with the board on a regular schedule enhances the relationship with the community and informs governing. This is somewhat different from community engagement, but is a highly recommended activity.

There are board members who regard public consultations as threatening to their control in the district, but school systems are not about control, they are about releasing potential. Genuine discussions between the school board and the community add authenticity to the claims of the school board as public representatives. The board's governance capacity (and its reputation) is also enhanced by regular avenues for interactive discussions—not board or superintendent monologues!

During these regular gatherings, relationships are built between the board and community members. People connect when they work together, dialogue becomes easier, discussion more focused, and participation increases. Additionally, as a result of regular discussions with community members, board members are usually in a very good situation to act confidently, and with the confidence of their community, when other levels of government surprise them with unexpected regulations or legislation that will affect the district operations. In this way, they know the culture of the school district, and can work within it.

SUMMARY

All school boards have a relationship with their communities, and with the people inside the school district. The culture of the district greatly influences that relationship. A school board that demonstrates strong leadership spends time and energy developing and maintaining a positive and interactive relationship with community members, and ensuring that the superintendent has created a culture of excellence for learning inside the district.

The potential for achieving a great school system lies in the vision, energy, community engagement, and collaboration of the board. Members must maintain their focus on governance—the real work of the board—and on democratic engagement.

School board members face the exceptional challenge of tapping into the hopes, dreams, and expectations of their constituencies so that they can, in turn, press those values into the local school district. School boards usually want to create cultures that value men, women, and children. It is the heart of what schools do: valuing people while shaping young lives.

A great learning culture is designed.

QUESTIONS

1. How would you describe the ideal school district culture?
2. Identify the indicators of this ideal culture.
3. What are some of the current issues in your community, and how could these suggest the real internal culture of the district?

APPLICATION

Take a sheet of paper, and at the top write out "The School District I See . . .", and then record at least ten qualities that would characterize the culture of your ideal school district. What would it take to have that list come true? What needs to change in policy or practice to make it happen?

NINE

Modeling Democracy

Leadership in Action

Influence reflects leadership. Some say that leadership is influence. The influence of school boards is most evident through the actions they take at the board table during public meetings. For most, it would be primarily to make rules and grant permissions. But the role of the school board is to lead and influence the school district toward a preferred future. How do tight rules and small permissions achieve that? The simple answer is that they rarely do. This chapter will explore the important ways school boards can actively lead their districts.

The governance function of the board specifies the distribution of responsibilities among different offices within the district, and spells out the rules and procedures for making decisions on corporate matters. School board members have to be deliberate and disciplined in ensuring that their work influences the district in the direction the board has agreed it will go, without interfering in the operations of the district.

In part, leadership means that board meetings should be mostly about goal achievement and policy review, because all the actions of the district, under the leadership of the superintendent, flow from the policies of the board. In this way, the responsibility to oversee and guide the school district is principally the responsibility of the school board. Board members who do not understand this discipline are often frustrated, but can learn how to lead properly.

Good governance is a product of how school districts are organized. This is explained in an organization chart. School boards and their placement in a bureaucratic hierarchy are not constructed to readily facilitate involvement in the school district, which is how it should be. This separation is often the cause for micromanaging. Board members do not recognize how the work they do at the board table enables the district to achieve its goals, and so they turn their focus instead to tangible (and usually administrative) matters that make them feel more involved.

However, positive board influence and guidance is readily achievable when the board and people who work with the board understand how to govern toward goals, and when board members refuse to engage in inappropriate behaviors by micromanaging matters. The board's responsibility is to oversee, assess progress, and direct the district corporate.

Recall that the singular purpose of the formal board meeting is to make decisions that cannot be made at any other level in the district organization. Board members need to be cognizant of the message they convey through their behavioral norms when meeting with or before the public, and adjust their habits to coincide with their stated values and vision.

Consider how uninviting most school board meetings are to the public. Typically, the district office has a room specifically dedicated to the meetings of the board, a formal room that communicates the seriousness of the proceedings that take place within its walls. In the boardroom, the board members sit behind desks (often in suits) with name plaques, binders, computers, and other paraphernalia that communicate clearly that they are more knowledgeable and much more important than anyone in the audience. Regardless of what school board members intend, the message is not inviting.

MINDFUL CONDUCT AT THE TABLE

Although board meetings are convened to accomplish business, formal meetings of the school board do seem to communicate that the public is not welcome. It is most distressing when the perception is reinforced by board member behavior.

Consider as an example the influence of these two actual board decisions on the operations of the entire school district. Each decision reflects the different mindsets of a school board toward governance and its purpose as a school board. The first decision is permission granted for a grade seven class in one elementary school to travel by school bus to the bowling lanes three miles from school. The second decision establishes a regular annual board consultation schedule for all identified school district interest groups.

These are very typical school board matters, and are excellent examples of good and poor leadership. The first decision involves the board in administrative matters that are beyond governance direction and control; the second decision reflects the board's desire for feedback from stakeholders on the district's progress in its strategy, which fuels the governance direction. At each public meeting of the school board, the board should receive feedback on the organization's progress and influence the upcoming decisions and activities of the district toward achievement of the district's objectives.

DISTINGUISHING BETWEEN TYPES OF POLICIES

Policies are, broadly, either administrative or governance. The first type guides the daily operational activities of the district; the second describes the work of the board. Key to the work of the superintendent is assuring the board that the administrative policies are appropriate to guiding the district toward its goals within acceptable parameters. The board ensures that its governance policies guide the district, but also guide the board itself in its work.

In former times, policies were highly detailed and restrictive. They tightly controlled behavior, and often reflected a problem of the era that was not solved at the school level. One example is an old policy that stated that the school board was not legally responsible for lost mittens; another referenced the stoking of the schoolhouse furnace.

In modern times, board policies try to reflect a confidence in the professionals within the school district. Most policies outline parameters of conduct, but allow freedom and appropriate applicability as situations demand. Policies that control and restrict reflect a board that does not have confidence in district professionals. Although this is rarely the intent of the board, it can be inherent in the wording and confines of the policy. One of the critical roles of the board members is to determine that the policy before them will enable and equip, rather than restrict and choke, a learning environment.

On those rare occasions when board members find themselves increasingly involved in controlling administrative matters, their lack of confidence may have valid justification, and the collection of data for presentation at the time of the superintendent's evaluation is appropriate and necessary. Most policies that control details deep within the organization, however, are a reflection of board members who do not understand governance, rather than of an overwhelmed superintendent.

The National School Boards Association has pioneered a policy catalog system that allows curious boards to reference similar policy areas of other districts to guide their policy development. Board members can search for school districts with similar missions and visions, and then examine their policies, modify them for their own situation, and benefit from the research and experience of other boards.

Chapter 9

DEVELOPING SCHOOL DISTRICT POLICY

One of the primary functions of the school board is to establish governance policies to guide the district. Many resources offer knowledge and coaching to board members who are unfamiliar with the purpose of policy and how to work with it. Taking the time to understand policy and its purposes is time well spent for school board members. It is through policy that the board speaks to the district and presents its overall corporate control and direction.

A comprehensive policy manual provides parameters for district decisions in the absence of the board. Ideally, there should be few policies, and mostly these should allow the superintendent much professional latitude and leadership. This allows for a fairer employment evaluation, and also demonstrates the confidence of the board in the district leadership.

Policies should really only state those matters that are not within the scope of the superintendent's responsibilities, such as how governance policies will be developed, a reflection and definition of the board's relationship with its community, and the board's overarching policies as an employer.

By leaving most administrative policies to the authority of the superintendent, board members are far more able to evaluate whether or not the everyday actions and culture of the district reflect the intended vision of the board. Board policies are intended to be broad because they oversee and direct the whole organization.

School boards can get caught up passing so many policies that, in the end, policies are ignored. Irrelevant policies, or an onerous number of policies, thwart the work of the district and the work of the board, because the board has no other legal way to communicate with the district. Board members need to be mindful of the fact that policy is only effective when it is utilized, and so must have their board policy manuals on a continuous review and assessment cycle. Policy manuals dormant on shelves communicate nothing except the irrelevance of the board.

Many school boards find ready justification in establishing many detailed policies, but in essence, a large policy manual invites board members to micromanage the organization. Board members who must approve policies want to be certain that they are relevant and sound. Since most policies typically are administrative, the board is formally invited into areas that are within the superintendent's general domain.

Another clear message from monstrously sized board manuals is that the board, not the superintendent, ultimately runs district administration and operations, and so, ultimately, no one is accountable. In these districts, the board is the final determinant in establishing tight rules, and is therefore responsible for their implementation.

For example, if the board is hiring school staff and there are problems, who is responsible for the bad hire? It cannot be the superintendent or principal or whoever, in fact, recommended the hire. Furthermore, numerous controlling and restrictive policies reflect a lack of trust in the professional capacities at all levels of the organization.

What is most important for school board members is to discern how the policy or proposal before them guides the district toward its goals, or if the policy proposed to them actually chokes the creativity and professionalism required for the effective delivery of education to students. The superintendent runs the district; the board, through policy, establishes the overall direction for the district.

WRITING EMPOWERING POLICY

Most policies are developed inside the school district and appear before the board as a recommendation. It is critical that when school boards are ready to vote, they have carefully considered the wording, intent, and measurability of the policy before them. Board governance policies are intended to guide the board, and to set an empowering direction for the administration of the district. A simple Internet search of online school board manuals will indicate that most school boards house every policy, rule, and regulation among the board policies. This invites micromanagement.

The policies of the school board need to guide the governance practices of the school board. For example, it may be the policy of the district to provide school bus transportation, and that will be what the board policy states. However, how many buses, the routes, who is eligible for the bus, and the times the routes run is *not* to be part of the board policy manual. These are administrative matters. If the district is not providing transportation to the satisfaction of the board, the board can ask the superintendent to explain why the action is as it is. This is governance, not micromanaging, and allows the board to provide input, but not make decisions.

Excellent board governance policies are best in a manual by themselves, often numbering somewhere between twenty and thirty policies. This way, the board members can review each of the policies throughout their term of service, on a regular cycle, to assure that the policies are still what the board needs to govern, and what the superintendent needs to administer the district.

In some of the strongest school districts, regulations and administrative matters are contained within an administrative manual, developed by the superintendent with those members in the employ of the district who are affected by the rules and regulations. This also helps the board to spend its time on governance, because it is not mired in administrative rules, the delivery and monitoring of which they have little control over. Administration is the purview of the superintendent, and when regulations need to be changed, they can be without going to the board.

Disempowering Policies

Some policies actually prohibit the development of a strong school community. Boards that insist on housing all the rules and policies of the district in its own manual tend to be overly involved in the daily administration of the district, and quickly disempower and discourage employees. Most school boards want their districts to be excellent, and want the professionals in the employment of the district to be focused on nurturing learning for all students. Innocently, though, board policies can have the opposite effect.

For example, many school boards have policies that demand frequent staffing changes in schools. There is the insistent argument that it is best for the professional development of teachers and administrators to change schools frequently, so boards comply and invoke this essentially administrative policy. Note that this type of policy proposal may serve some interests, but may not reflect the overall corporate direction. Board members need to ask themselves why the policy is like this: School communities cannot be strong if the leaders are constantly threatened with abrupt job changes.

If the priority of the board is teacher change, the policy may reflect its vision. If the priority of the board is stable learning communities, the purpose of such a policy should be questioned. Policies are established to equip, empower, direct, or control. They must not contradict district purpose or vision. This is also a good example of a board policy that perhaps would be most suitable as an administrative rule, so that the board can ask the superintendent to account for these choices.

Board members need to be very mindful of the full impact of policies that they are prepared to implement. The board, not the administrators, will have to justify its policy to sometimes angry or disappointed school communities, or to distressed families and ratepayers. Using the example above, those boards that do have policies mandating school changes usually do not have the same mandate for the senior administrative positions. This does not make sense.

If it is best for learning environments and professional development to enforce change every three to four years, then the same principles should apply to all members of the district—including the superintendent and every board member. Boards need to insist that all of their policies provide overall corporate direction consistent with the vision of education they have crafted through honing community values during consultation. Remember, these decisions also influence the culture of the district, which also impacts learning.

QUESTIONS TO ASK ABOUT POLICY RECOMMENDATIONS

The objective of good school board governance is the promotion of strong and effective school districts. By selecting and employing the right superintendent, the board makes its greatest contribution to the district. In addition, the board's involvement in policy development reflects the governance tradition that board members provide oversight, insight, and foresight, rather than micromanagement of the district. This is most keenly communicated through board policies and decisions taken at the board table.

The watchful, sober second thought of board members is critical when examining policy proposals. There are a handful of principles to guide questions and considerations that will assist board members to stay within their mandated governance capacities, and help them to produce policies that give direction to the district without inhibiting the leadership of the superintendent or other district leaders.

Board members are active in high-level school district matters primarily through the types of questions that they ask when they are convened as a board. Critical questions for effective governance include those that focus the discussion back on the direction of the district, the capacity of the district, the mission and vision of the district, and the internal ethical and cultural priorities of the district.

A strong governing board also inquires about the clarity of objectives in a proposed policy. That is, the policy must not be ambiguous regarding what is being accomplished, it must be measurable (to allow for determination of achievement), and it must be both timely and acceptable in terms of the district's vision and values.

Public policy is exactly that: It sets rules and direction for a public administration toward objectives articulated and determined on behalf of the public. School board policies are public policies.

CONSULTATION

Consultations influence policy. Consultation is a term that is culturally defined; that is, it has different meanings for different boards and board members and, as discussed earlier, is different from community engagement, and is much narrower.

Elected members need to be confident that the version of consultation practiced by their board is sufficient for the populations they serve. Most communities appreciate and expect broader democratic engagement. A brief scan of education reform suggests that education policies that improve education are contentious, and so consultation is critical to gain support and understanding when the board must implement changes that will produce questions from its communities.

There are two ends of the consultation spectrum. At one end, the board stays in control, drafts a policy regarding a specific area, and asks targeted interest groups to approve it. Convinced that they have done the due diligence required for consultation, the board approves the recommended policy with minor changes. This is a top-down model, and the final product rarely reflects accommodation of contributing parties.

At the other end, and more in keeping with the current educational leadership literature and community engagement literature, the board recognizes consultation as a tool to develop organizational purposes and to improve education policy. In this consultation model, the board establishes regular discussions with stakeholders, some of which might include policy development sessions.

Policy development in this latter model involves reflection, examination, criticizing, accommodating, reformulating, and testing the intuitive understandings of a problem or situation. Sometimes the process does not result in a policy, but it does build a culture conducive to adaptation and leadership at all levels.

POLICY REVIEW

Finally, board members need to be familiar with policy, and this means regular review. If the district follows a good governance model, in which the board is only responsible for governance policies, a regular schedule of review and monitoring policy achievements keeps the board closely focused on governance. If the board retains a very large manual, regular review and scrutiny is even more critical to assure compliance. While reviewing the policies, board members must determine if the policy is still guiding, measuring, and achieving what it is intended to do.

When the district combines administrative policies with governance policies, the board has hundreds of policies to review and monitor, but this is also manageable with a competent superintendent. Since policies guide the district activities, it is imperative that board members understand whether or not the policies they approve facilitate or thwart the achievement of the vision the board has set for the district.

SUMMARY

Leadership in action for school board members has a lot to do with their role as policy makers. In that role, consultation is not a checklist of who has read the proposed policy, but is a mechanism of empowerment, information processing, improvement, and ultimately, respect. When school boards receive a recommendation for policy that has been nurtured and developed from the source of implementation, the board is often approving a request for guidance through policy, rather than imposing a policy on the organization.

Policy review and development alerts the board to when it is staying on course, and when it needs to adjust. Active leadership on the school board, by each and every member, requires diligence, prioritizing, careful thought, and focus. Leadership that produces excellent guiding policies, which, in turn, produce strong track records, is one of the most rewarding facets of school board membership.

QUESTIONS

1. Why do rules and permissions restrict community engagement?
2. What are the main differences between consultation and community engagement?
3. What are some of the ways that policy development and implementation can weaken the governance function of the board?

APPLICATION

Write a policy to ensure meaningful and ongoing policy review and development. How does your policy uphold the role of the school board and the goals of the district? How would you measure the effectiveness of your policy?

TEN
Administering Democracy

The Superintendent and CEO

There is, perhaps, no single person more able to influence every facet of a school district—as a chief advocate for children, for education professionals, and for the future of educational achievement—than the superintendent. As chief executive officer, the superintendent is also a highly qualified management expert, offering a unique blend of corporate competencies and educational expertise to the executive management of the school district.

The school board collects the values of its community and filters those, through the work of the superintendent, into the schools. The superintendent, as an education and organizational professional, is responsible for ensuring that the district is providing the best education for students that it can, within the parameters set by the school board. This vision is developed through community engagement, consultation, and representation.

There are many sources of literature about the import of the board-superintendent relationship, and those who are interested in school board governance and the role of the school board would be well served to understand as much as they can about the nature and nurture of this pivotal relationship. In short, the entire school district bears the handprint of the superintendent, and it is through the superintendent that the board presses local values into the school system.

Board members must recognize that the superintendent fills a unique and critical role in the district as the CEO and leader of the district, but also as chief advisor and conduit to the organization for the board. Boards with great superintendents have learned how to communicate value to the superintendent, and refrain from involving themselves in his/her work.

The superintendent works for the board. The board corporate is responsible for hiring, evaluating and, if necessary, parting company with the superintendent when his or her leadership style and direction do not reflect local values. Almost without exception, superintendents are the board's most valuable resource. Through the superintendent, visions are turned into reality, problems are solved, budgets are planned, schools are positive places of learning, and learning takes place through innovative, effect measures.

Boards with superintendents who are strong and effective leaders find themselves quite easily in the part-time governance role they are intended to fill. As the board's key and only employee, the superintendent is an excellent planner, facilitator, communicator, motivator, and problem solver.

In most school districts, the superintendent is admired and respected by the board, the community, and by employees within the district organization. Weak or overwhelmed superintendents are rare, but when they are evidenced, board members must find the fortitude required to work with the superintendent for a finite period of time, at the end of which, without sufficient improvement, the superintendent and district part company.

Good superintendents motivate their staffs and have acquired the respect of their communities and their board members through an admirable track record of a continuously improving school district. Their energy and vision is compatible with the vision determined by the board to reflect the will of the community, and each year, board members see that vision manifesting itself before their eyes, as education, morale, student learning, and even mundane tasks inside the district reflect the passion and excellence of the district's senior executive officer.

WORKING WITH THE BOARD

People have different motivations, and school board members are no different. Understanding motivations is a key leadership factor for superintendents, and in school board governance. Board member motivations often explain the politics of the board table. One of the unique qualities of board governance, though, is the requirement for all board members to support the recorded decisions of the majority.

It can be particularly difficult for the superintendent if board members lack respect for one another. And the credibility of the school board is seriously eroded when personality clashes are evident in public meetings. The media is quick to report any conflict displayed among school board members, and so board members should really consider methods to help them understand one another.

For superintendents and for board chairs, understanding the personalities around the board table facilitates meeting planning. As outlined in chapter 5, many reliable personality assessment tools are available, and the use of one or more assists the board members as they work together. Often, board members feel unimportant or undervalued, and learning how to communicate value provides moral support and encouragement, and improves relationships at the board table overall.

Relationships are critical at the board table. Board chairs and superintendents who understand that board members need to feel that they are making valuable contributions to the board find guidance and understanding for the difficult tasks of resolving conflict or of receiving support for a recommendation in these relationships. It is not uncommon for board members who feel undervalued by their colleagues to refuse to support a good recommendation for the district, especially if they will be seen as agreeing with board members by whom they feel alienated or disliked. This harms the district, and does not repair any relationship.

Personality profiling can be an important and useful tool to facilitate effective board table discussions and decisions and, when recognized and utilized by skilled board chairs, can minimize board strife and improve board action and activity. School boards must plot the future direction of the district, and are crippled in their efforts if relationships between the board members, and between the board and the superintendent, are adversarial.

Superintendents are extremely well qualified for their positions, and bring expertise, education, and experience to the district that only a handful of other people in the country can offer. The superintendent is the CEO of the school district. Governance, by nature, involves some overlap, but effective school boards determine which decisions are to be made by the board, and which decisions are to be made by the superintendent, and work hard to respect this division of labor.

Through regular policy review, boards can change their determination of which key decisions and judgments must be made by the board, and which are to be made by the superintendent. Those decisions that are the superintendent's need to be respected, and reviewed as part of his or her accountability and evaluation criteria when the board is performing its evaluation of the superintendent's performance.

The superintendent's position in the organization is always to be respected by board members and by people within the organization. Some people inside the district will try to circumvent the superintendent and communicate directly with board members. In most circumstances, this is not particularly sinister; in others, it is a desperate plea for help or assistance.

Board members must always be diligent in distinguishing between their role as citizen representatives and the superintendent's role as head of the organization. Employees who complain to the board are out of line; citizens who complain to the board are within their democratic rights. This is a challenging distinction for most board members. However, if there is an area within the organization requiring board audit, even if it is the leadership style of the superintendent, there are other means of identifying such problems, and there are appropriate means of evaluating the work of the superintendent.

EXCEPTIONAL LEADERSHIP

Literature identifies great leadership qualities that are applicable to school districts with exceptional superintendents. These qualities are identified in management literature as reasons why some organizations grow, and why others stagnate. Most superintendents represent the reason for the presence or the absence of these outstanding organizational characteristics.

Organizations that continually make right changes grow and expand their capacities and accomplishment in a spiral that winds continuously upward and outward. In school districts such as these, there is an energy—an excitement—throughout the organization that captures the hearts and minds of all who come into contact with it.

These organizations also have a quality of excellence that has been identified as progressive. That is, they do not just aim to be excellent at the end of a term or a specified period; every day they do their very best. Excellence is a continuous, daily pursuit and habit. People in school districts like these are enthusiastic and expectant. Rarely are there employees or even students with low energy. Such organizations as these are never concerned about their budgets.

For school districts like these, value for money is recognized, employees are prudent, and citizens are not resentful or accusing the district of waste. These organizations include everyone and have mission statements that ignite and excite, so that all people within the organization and in contact with it are extremely motivated and eager to apply their knowledge.

For school systems, this type of leadership launches potential and possibilities like no other. There is a sense of conviction that the work of the organization will change the next generation, and this dynamic sentiment provides opportunities for students that would never even emerge in the minds of people caught in a lesser organization. Exceptional leaders lead school districts into the preferred future that the public hopes to see.

The superintendent has the training and expertise, and usually the vision, to achieve goals and pursue excellence in education delivery, while the board provides governance and cultivates community values. The leadership of the superintendent is critical to the work of the school district. It is the responsibility of the board to ensure that the right leader for the right time is at the helm of the school district.

THE BUDGET AS A LEADERSHIP TOOL

Where there is public money, there are bureaucratic budget processes. A huge annual task for the superintendent is the development and establishment of the annual operating budget. A general understanding of current trends in fiscal management is valuable to the school board, especially as it strives to provide effective leadership in this sometimes confusing, yet critical area of governance. Budgets can provide value as a management planning tools for school boards, but only if board members know how to use them and which information to request.

One of the challenges for school district administrators is the scrutiny of the budget by the members of the board. In this area, board members often step well out of their governance role and meddle in matters where they typically lack knowledge, qualification, or expertise. The presentation of the proposed budget often involves the production of large binders containing line items and corresponding dollar amounts, a presentation to the elected board members, and then the lengthy study of the items by the board.

Questioning the district administration about proposed expenditures is a form of accountability, but typically board members are caught up in questions that are not governance questions. The budget process provides ready opportunities for board members to inadvertently step into the jobs of qualified personnel within the school district.

For example, board members will debate the number of buses to be purchased (which is within the responsibilities of the superintendent, and often delegated several levels below the superintendent), rather than determining whether or not previous allocations for buses are meeting the goals established in prior budgets. The question for board members should not be "How many buses?" but rather "Do we require buses to achieve the goals we have set for our district?" The questions board members pose to the district administration should be governance-based and assist the district to continuously focus outward to the people it serves.

Public sector budget procedures clarify the leadership potential for school boards. Traditional budget making at the federal level, until the late 1960s, was the incremental line-item budget fairly typical of today's school districts. The line-item budget is a line-by-line list of objects of expenditure over a specific year. Such a budget is relatively easy to draft for middle managers, and poses no serious challenges to the superintendency.

However, this budget style is not conducive to justifying or defending the purposes and interests of the expenditure proposals. Since there is really very scant information provided to the board, the line-item budget is not very effective as a planning or evaluation tool. Despite the complexity and size of the budget, it provides elected officials with only a limited ability to assess and evaluate the quality of work being sustained through the proposed expenditures.

This type of budget tends to be from the bottom up, but only in the sense that it moves from the administrative level to the governance level, and really does not allow the superintendent to adequately express his or her passions or initiatives. The budget itself does not provide information to measure effectiveness or allow for an assessment of how efficiently resources are being used.

Although it has been more than thirty years since the federal public service abandoned line-item budgeting, school boards still rely on it almost exclusively. Instead, school boards could request budget documents that would allow them to debate leadership matters, rather than a document that allows them to second-guess the hard work of the administration.

More popular in the social services of the public sector has been the integration of management and performance monitoring. Although these systems have presented many challenges to politicians and public servants at all levels of government, they do provide boards with clearly defined and available results.

Typically, budget processes are intimidating to some board members, and a source of self-importance to others who like to pounce on details and insist on what are ultimately tiny tweaks to a multimillion-dollar budget. As public representatives, though, the information that board members really require from the district administration is the general emphasis of spending and the overall number of dollars.

How the budget is presented to the board is the discretionary call of the superintendent and the chief financial officer of the district, but often it is in a package that invites tremendous micromanaging and questions that are well below the level of governance. It is right for board members to know how much money the superintendent intends to spend on lunches for his team over the upcoming year, because he reports directly to the board, but there is no need for board members to judge how many dollars are allocated for construction paper in a grade one classroom.

All school district budgets must comply with accepted federal and state accounting practices, and it is the job of the superintendent to ensure that this happens. A superintendent who understands the thought processes and priorities of board members can usually produce a better presentation for the board than they can ask for themselves. This management expertise is one of the reasons why the board has a superintendent in its employ.

The superintendent and other district leaders are paid to determine how much money is needed for which areas; board members need to provide a mission, and to audit budget proposals to ensure that the district is appropriately resourced to achieve established goals.

How the budget is presented to the public is the decision of the board, and a board in regular and effective communication with its constituency finds important and creative ways to do this. Budget proposals that demonstrate spending allocations in a traditional pie chart usually provide the information that members of the public and members of the board can understand and discuss.

There is no need for board members or for members of the public to debate how much money is projected for photocopying and other details of office life, for example. But they would like to know, for example, how much of the budget is spent on administrative costs. Providing information in simple categories is much more conducive to building trust between the district, the board, and the public. It also provides a visual statement of board priorities that prompts responses from the public regarding priorities reflected in the proposed budget.

Traditional bureaucratic management has provided a long history of thick, detailed, budget books that do not provide the transparency and honesty that most boards or administrations think they provide. It is the responsibility of the board to ensure that it is communicating with citizens in terms that are understandable and fairly measurable. The public has many creative ways of communicating their disagreement to the board over proposed budgets.

LEADERSHIP AND SUCCESSION PLANNING

Planning is critical to good governance, and careful planning for the top position of the school district—the superintendent—is critical. School boards must always have plans so that they can succeed at their work. Often school boards govern reactively, or even retroactively, but governance, by nature, is forward-oriented. Plans allow the board to control its behavior and its goals, and grant confidence that at the end of the board's term, the members will have made a positive, measured difference in the progress of the district.

There is a new trend in public service away from the strategic plans that gripped school districts through the last two decades. Strategic plans are excellent tools, and for many leaders, they chart a course and keep the organization moving toward its goals. They provide superintendents with ready evidence of achieved goals and continuous improvement.

For many of today's maverick superintendents, the strategic plan develops organically as a response to the board's relationship with its constituency. As the board reviews its policies and debates its current governing relevance and purpose, the superintendent is given the freedom required to pursue his or her leadership goals for the district.

These school boards find that their most strategic efforts are made through public conversations, and they expend their energy listening and dialoguing with the public, so that they can mediate between the superintendent's professional opinions and goals, and the values of the communities served by the district schools.

School boards with momentum want to maintain their steady march of continued district improvement. Just as the board looks to the future to define its vision, so it must be prepared when changes to the human composition of the district leadership are on the horizon.

Planning for a new superintendent is a critical task for school boards. The superintendent is the singular greatest influence on the culture, composition, structure, and morale of the district, all of which, according to research, directly impact student learning. Some superintendents are very skilled at developing other leaders, and so there are people within the district who have been nurtured to one day fill the superintendent's job.

Board members are wisest when they are absolutely assured that the choice that they have finally made is the best fit for their district, and for the direction the district is heading. This process is not a simple one, and well beyond the capabilities of most school board members. The process of hiring a superintendent requires the investment of time, resources, and a professional who can guide the board and district through the process.

The board that can engage its community and its employees, and follow the guidance of a trained professional recruiter, rarely chose an inappropriate replacement. Other boards have followed their own ideas and feelings for recruiting a new superintendent/CEO, with very serious implications for the district.

There is a true story of a board that appointed a superintendent based on false information provided by the previous school board, and indicators of competence that included sending hand-signed birthday cards to 1,100+ district employees. When it was time to negotiate the contract with the new superintendent, the board was shocked to find a professional negotiator across the table, while the superintendent-designate remained in communication with the negotiator—not the board—by telephone. This board had no process.

In another situation, two neighboring boards followed the advice of professional executive recruiters, but they were also engaged in positive relationships with their communities. They produced a transparent process that included the careful, detailed input of staff, parent councils, many community members, and included the outgoing superintendent.

By implementing wise governance principles, the boards were able to continue their consistent district growth through the transition in leadership. Succession planning is one of the most critical functions of the elected school board. The superintendent is the leader of the district and in charge of how the district works and how it attains its vision.

Board members must be very careful not to interfere in the work of this critical, valued, and superior employee. The fact is, the superintendent is preeminently responsible for everything that takes place inside the school district, from its culture to employee performance. The task of the board is to evaluate whether this is taking place within the culture, goals, and expectations of the school board.

QUESTIONS

1. What are the general expectations of the role of a school district superintendent? How is this different from the role of a school board, and a school board member?
2. Review your board policy manual. How does it reflect the core principles of leadership as outlined in this chapter?
3. Why is succession planning an important role of the school board?

APPLICATION

Make a list of the leadership strengths of the superintendent/CEO of your school district. Include instances of how these strengths have been evidenced, and then send him or her a note of appreciation.

Conclusion

Leading Democracy: The Governing School Board

King Solomon said there is a time for everything under the sun; so it is with school board leadership. There is a time to build leadership capacity, and there is a time to exercise leadership. There is also a time to engage with the community, to ensure the relationships within the district are positive, to nurture learning. Those habits, relationships, and policies that are developed and practiced during non-crisis periods of school board governance are those that will serve the board and superintendent well during difficult times, and these routines produce exceptional results for education.

School boards and school districts serve our students in an environment of challenges and difficulties that are increasingly imposed on them from external authorities. While some might argue that school boards have brought these intrusions on themselves by retreating from competence in the past, current school board members are evidencing a commitment to meet these challenges head on, maintain a focus on a clear vision for the future, and adapt where they must to provide sound governance for school districts.

There is much literature outlining the qualities of successful, effective, and high-impact school boards. Understanding the premises of this literature, and applying it at the board table, builds habits that will be the strength of the board. These habits and guiding principles allow the board to lead with purpose, and foster public respect through the trials and difficulties that are part of the normal life cycle of the modern school board.

However, poor habits may sabotage good decisions. As an example of such a situation, there was a Midwestern school board that had a contentious relationship with its citizens, parents, and parent councils. When the board wanted to make a change that research indicated was truly a sound educational decision, even the state leadership stood against the board. The board had not developed relationships, communication patterns, and trust with its community or with its education partners, and so a decision that was perhaps a better structure for students became another fracture in the tumultuous track record of this school board. Community engagement, and the resulting trust, is important for school boards to do the work they are required to do.

Boards can never underestimate the compelling power of sound leadership, good habits, respectful governance, and routine decisions that build public confidence. School board leadership that is trusted because of its community relationships enables the board to move forward with the engaged support of its communities when there are difficult and even unpopular decisions on the table.

RIGHTS, DEMOCRACY, AND THE PUBLIC SCHOOL

America is rooted in the democratic value of responsibility for one another. Fundamentally, this is why we have school boards. School boards are responsible to the rest of society for ensuring that the school districts are well run and do not operate in ways that are counterproductive to the goals and values of the communities they serve.

In the current age of the rights dialogue, board members are often conflicted by multiple demands on their decision-making accomplishments, and are often asked to choose between rights and responsibilities. Although the American Bill of Rights and other legislation has occasionally presented challenges to school boards, these challenges have usually resulted in a society more deeply rooted in the values of life and liberty.

Pressure exerted on school boards from different rights groups may, at times, be intimidating, but when board members have a clear vision of the future school district, and a clear understanding of the legislation that governs them and the public values that guide them, they are usually able to auger through controversy and make the decision that best reflects their public responsibilities and confirms their respected role in the community. Schools in a democratic state exist to teach the young how to live together and build society respectfully. Without respectful responsibility to build society together, democracy, and the schools it requires, will fail.

THE INDICATORS OF SUCCESS

At the end of the day, board members know whether or not they are members of an effective board that governs a successful district. Board members know in their hearts whether they are doing a good job. Board members know whether or not employees are happy; whether or not the schools are resourced properly, and whether or not they have the right superintendent leading the district. They know whether their citizenry is exasperated with them or has a quiet confidence in the work they do.

For those boards that want to improve their governance, there are numerous excellent measurement instruments readily available for school boards. School board-related organizations such as the National School Boards Association offer many tools and much training for willing board members. Local school boards are in the best position to determine which one or ones they should use; individual board members know which skills they need to hone and, again, much assistance is available.

The real success of a school board is found in its ability to demonstrate its central purpose through consistently good governance decisions. School boards oversee district administration and education delivery to ensure that the heartfelt views and opinions of the public are recognizable in the school system. Members of strong boards understand which decision areas constitute corporate decisions, and are therefore board decisions, and which decision areas are operational or management decisions belonging to the superintendent.

Board members closely tuned to their communities tend to be those who are involved with their communities, not preoccupied evening after evening chairing internal district committee meetings over matters that are not governance matters. To press local values into the schools, board members need to know what those values are, and they are far more likely to acquire them at the community hockey rink, in the stands at the football games, among the lawn chairs at soccer and baseball tournaments, and through chance encounters at the local store.

The purpose of a school board in American democracy is to engage the communities it serves and represents, so that it may press local values into the schools. Board members know whether or not their voting patterns reflect the will of their communities, or whether they are continuously forcing incompatible policy and direction down the throats of the citizenry that support, fund, and entrust tomorrow's society to the decisions of the school board.

Many school board members can effectively and evidentially answer the question, "What is different and improved in this district since we came to office?" There are many others who will look to the accomplishments of their superintendent and staff, and cite those, because as a board, their contributions have been merely permissions and restrictive controls.

The board has to recognize that its job is not performed by any other office in the school district. The role of the board is multifaceted, and although governing does have some overlap, for the most part, the board's role is distinct and simple. This is, perhaps, where boards have lost their way over the decades. School board members are elected to represent the community, most members of which are not educational or organizational experts. Board members must not only want to *be* fine leaders, they must be *willing to be* fine leaders.

The board ensures that the district has a superintendent who solicits the best, not just in terms of academic qualifications, but also in employees who will build community, trust, fairness, and justice in the daily school experience. These are some of the most precious values of our society, and those we expect to see authentically present in modern school districts.

Sometimes board members forget that there are professional societies, universities, employment unions, and private consultants that protect areas such as teacher welfare, employment fairness, professional qualifications, etc. Board members simply need to concern themselves with whether they have a clear vision of where the district should be in the future, and whether the superintendent in the employ of the board can do the job acceptably.

The superintendent's role is very powerful, and has a far greater immediate effect on the district than any school board does, yet the influence and effect of the superintendent as the district leader is also the responsibility of the board. When the board thoroughly understands the expectations of its constituencies for the district, the determination of the suitability of the superintendent is not difficult.

Through the superintendent, the entire district takes shape. Schools develop their cultures, attract students and staff, engage their communities, and empower their parent councils beyond fund-raising to engage in meaningful school promotion under the leadership of the superintendent. District offices, principals, educators, and specialists motivate, encourage, heal, contribute, and think under the primary leadership of the superintendent.

Resources are expended, buildings are built, renovated, and sold, buses are purchased and scheduled, and even parking lots are paved under the leadership of the superintendent. The book of board policies and the minutes of public board meetings are all recommended, transcribed, and published through the office of the superintendent. There is no one more critical to the democratic values of the school system than the superintendent—except the board that pays close professional and communal attention to the effect of the superintendent on the entire organization and its outcomes.

Although there are many useful and effective tools for measuring success, school board members know whether they are doing the job they were elected to do. Professional measurement instruments assist them in the legitimization of what they already know to be true. Whether board members choose to use the information they have to take action toward improvement is their own ethical decision, and ultimately should provide evidence for their return to office or their retirement.

As Stanford University researcher Jim Collins has said through his *Good to Great* studies, the wrong people cannot be motivated to do the right thing. The responsibility to employ the right superintendent is the paramount responsibility of the board; the responsibility to elect the right board is the democratic responsibility of each voter.

LEADERSHIP

Recent trends in education research and organization theory are built upon the open systems model, in which inputs are transformed by an organization into outputs. For school systems, students are the important input drawn from the environment; outputs include transformed students, a learning culture, drop-out rates, literacy and numeracy rates, even such traditionally immeasurable outputs as excellence, positive culture and constant improvement.

For school boards, the open systems model allows a fairer and more community-minded assessment of district accomplishments, while respecting the skill and knowledge inherent in today's professional learning communities and professional educators.

Structure and culture, for example, are key transformational factors of an open organizational system, as are the shared orientations of an organization's population. Community vision, of course, is the shared orientation of the school board. School boards have the authority and responsibility to alter both the structure and culture of a school district toward the vision they have developed in collaboration with their community.

Thus, school districts requiring improved library facilities or facing escalating transportation costs can move beyond the traditional policy instrument of in-house provision, or of contracting out, and instead partner with other municipal services to provide the services schools require at lesser costs. School boards can move outside the bureaucratic structures and theories that have held educational improvement hostage, and achieve district goals by focusing as much on the transformational elements of the district organization as they do on stated goals or outcomes.

Trends in administration and governance offer a plethora of creative options for school board members. Networking, partnerships, leveraging the community strength of parent councils, and the reinventing government movement provide opportunities for effective governance to meet the needs and demands of modern school districts. School board members have the chance to move beyond the traditions of less effective governance and build improved school districts that habitually innovate, continually improve their performance, and change the minds of critics.

SUMMARY

Education leadership and governance is a fascinating field. Critical research, theories, and findings feed the hunger of our professional educators to meet the learning needs of today's students with ever-improving methodologies. For the intellectually curious board member, there are relevant resources regarding leadership available for the asking.

But school board members highly trained in educational administration, pedagogy, and curriculum are not what the country needs. We need school board members who can link into their communities, understand the dream within, articulate it into a vision, and communicate those values through the superintendent into the daily operations of the district. When board members think that they need to be educational experts in order to govern, they begin to drift off course from the fulfillment of their role on the school board.

The school board contribution is unique and vital in American democracy; where the future leads is up to those who serve on our school boards, and the people who elect them. School boards are at the crossroads of collapse and triumph. There are many resources available to tell people how to become school board members. There are even more telling them how to be effective.

This book has presented the reasons America has believed in school boards and established them as the most immediate form of democracy. Hopefully it has motivated readers to support and compel school boards and board members to fulfill their primary and exclusive purpose in our school systems. If everyone who comprises the democratic educational community seizes the opportunities before us to return school boards to their critical and relevant function, education in America will soar to heights we only dream of.

The potential for greatness is there. Education is extremely important to our society and to our democracy. Educators are excellent; they are the best in history. The country is healthy; there are tax dollars, resources, and a sincere desire across the nation to nurture our young students to their maximum potential. The vehicle that can stymie the dream for educators, parents, ratepayers, politicians, and even students, is the well-intended but underperforming school board, whose members intend to make a difference, but simply do not.

American dreams can come to life through well-governed school boards. No other democratically established body can engage, empower, and build community the way school boards can, one member at a time. Boards equip and entrust districts to do the work they are professionally trained to do, while demonstrating leadership and governance. School boards can aggressively understand their role in the oversight, insight, and foresight required to assure the preservation of local values in the delivery of education in our schools.

Excellent school systems are the byproduct of excellent governors elected by their communities to represent and empower them in ways that nothing but the tenets of democracy can guarantee. This can take a while, but results come from resolving to follow the routines of solid policy, authentic community engagement, and excellent governance. The processes of democracy are simple, and school boards, entrusted with the future of society, are uniquely established to set the example for all levels of government. All board members need to do is to understand the democratic plan for school boards, and bring the intentions to life.

The resolve to have great school systems without the resolve to adhere to the tenets of good governance cannot yield the results we long to achieve. This is the unique and necessary contribution to society that only school boards can uphold. And it is the hope school boards offer their communities. School board members need to lift their eyes to the horizon and keep their focus there and, in this era of community-engaged governance, guard our trust with strong leadership.

Bibliography

Adsit, Tim. *Small Schools, Education, and the Importance of Community: Pathways to Improvement and a Sustainable Future*. Lanham, MD: Rowman & Littlefield Education, 2011.
Babbage, Keen. *Reform Doesn't Work: Grassroots Efforts Can Provide Answers to School Improvement*. Lanham: Rowman & Littlefield Education, 2012.
Baker, Eva L. "The end(s) of testing." *Educational Researcher* 36, no. 7 (August/September 2007): 309–317.
Bart, Chris. *20 Questions Directors Should Ask about Strategy*. Toronto: Canadian Institute of Chartered Accountants, 2003.
Blanchard, Ken, B. Hybels, and Phil Hodges. *Leadership by the Book: Tools to Transform Your Workplace*. New York: William Morrow and Company Inc., 1999.
Burch, Patricia. "Educational Policy and Practice from the Perspective of Institutional Theory: Crafting a Wider Lens." *Educational Researcher* 34, no. 2 (March 2007): 84–95.
Canadian School Boards Association. http://www.cdnsba.org.
Carnegie Foundation for the Advancement of Teaching. http://cdn.carnegiefoundation.org.
Chapman, Gary, and Paul White. *The 5 Languages of Appreciation in the Workplace: Empowering Organizations by Encouraging People*. Chicago: Northfield Publishing, 2012.
Collins, Jim. *Good to Great*. New York: HarperCollins Publishers Inc., 2001.
———. *Good to Great and the Social Sectors*. Boulder, CO: Jim Collins, 2005.
Danzberger, Jacqueline P. "Governing the Nation's Schools: The Case for Restructuring Local School Boards." *Phi Kappa Delta* 75 (1994): 367.
Dawson, Linda D., and Randy Quinn. "Moving Boards Out of Operations, Into Results." *School Administrator* 58, no. 3 (March 2001): 54.
Dewey, John. *Democracy and Education*. Charleston, SC: Bibliobazaar, 2007.
Drucker, Peter. *The Five Most Important Questions You Will Ever Ask About Your Organization*. San Francisco: Jossey-Bass, 2008.
Dumlao, Rebecca, and Emily Janke. "Using Relational Dialectics to Address Differences in Community-Campus Partnerships." *Journal of Higher Education Outreach and Engagement*, no. 2 (2012): 79–103.
Eadie, Doug. *Extraordinary Board Leadership: The Seven Keys to High-Impact Governance*. Gaithersburg, MD: Aspen Publishers, 2001.
———. *Five Habits of High-Impact School Boards*. Lanham, MD: Rowman & Littlefield Education, 2005.
Edelman, Murray. *Words that Work: Policies that Fail*. Madison: University of Wisconsin Press, 1977.
Gaskell, Jane. "The 'Public' in Public Schools: A School Board Debate." *Canadian Journal of Education* 26, no. 1 (2001): 19–36.
Gerald, Kevin. *By Design or Default: Creating a Church Culture that Works*. Nashville, TN: Thomas Nelson Inc., 2006.
Goodlad, John, and Timothy J. McMannon, eds. *The Public Purpose of Education and Schooling*. San Francisco: Jossey-Bass Publishers, 1997.
Hamilton, Lynn. *The Secrets of School Board Success: Practical Tips for Board Members*. Lanham, MD: Rowman & Littlefield Education, 2007.
Hardy, Larry. "Change Happens." *American School Board Journal* (January 2008).

Bibliography

Houston, Paul, and Doug Eadie. *The Board-Savvy Superintendent*. Lanham, MD: Rowman and Littlefield Publishing, 2002.

Kretzmann, John P., and John McKnight. *Building Communities from the Inside Out: A Path Toward Finding and Mobilizing a Community's Assets*. Chicago: ACTA Publications, 1993.

Lee, Blaine. *The Power Principle: Influence with Honor*. New York: Covey Leadership Center Inc., 1997.

Leithwood, Kenneth, and Steinbach, Rosanne. *Expert Problem Solving: Evidence from School and District Leaders*. Albany, NY: University of New York Press, 1995.

Leithwood, K., D. Jantzi, and R. Steinbach. "Changing Leadership for Changing Times." *Journal of Education for Teaching: International Research and Pedagogy* 26, no. 2 (July 2000): 189–199.

Lieberman, Myron. *The Educational Morass: Overcoming the Stalemate in American Education*. Lanham, MD: Rowman & Littlefield Education, 2007.

Maxwell, John C. *Developing the Leader Within You*. Nashville: Thomas Nelson, 1993.

———. *Developing the Leaders Around You: How to Help Others Reach Their Full Potential*. Nashville: Thomas Nelson, 1995.

———. *Ethics 101: What Every Leader Needs to Know*. New York: Center Street Books, 2003.

McAdams, Donald R. *What School Boards Can Do: Reform Governance for Urban Schools*. New York: Teachers College Press, 2006.

National School Boards Association. http://www.nsba.org

Narayan, D., ed. *Empowerment and Poverty Reduction: A Sourcebook*. Washington, DC: World Bank, 2002.

New England Research Center for Higher Education. http://www.nerche.org.

Osborne, David, and Peter Plastrik. *Banishing Bureaucracy: The Five Strategies for Reinventing Government*. Reading, MA: Addison-Wesley Publishing Company, 1997.

Ouchi, William G. *Making Schools Work: A Revolutionary Plan to Get Your Children the Education They Need*. New York: Simon & Schuster, 2003.

Reimer, Laura. *Leadership and School Boards: Guarding the Trust*. Lanham, MD: Rowman & Littlefield Education, 2008.

Rivers, Ian, Neil Duncan, and Valerie Besag. *Bullying: A Handbook for Educators and Parents*. Lanham, MD: Rowman & Littlefield Education, 2009.

Saltmarsh, J., M. Hartley, and P. Clayton. *Democratic Engagement White Paper*. Boston: New England Resource Center for Higher Education, 2009.

Saltmarsh, J., and M. Hartley. *To Serve a Larger Purpose: Engagement for Democracy and the Transformation of Higher Education*. Philadelphia: Temple University Press, 2011.

Savoie, Donald. "Searching for Accountability in a World Without Boundaries," *Canadian Public Administration* 47, no. 1 (Spring 2004): 1–26.

Scanlon, Paul. *Without a Complaint Your Vision Will Perish* [electronic version]. Bradford, UK: ALM, 2007.

———. *Crossing Over: Getting to the Best Life Ever*. Bradford, UK: ALM, 2007.

Schaef, Anne Wilson, and Fassel, Diane. *The Addictive Organization*. New York: HarperCollins Publishers, 1988.

Schmoker, Mike. *Results: The Key to Continuous School Improvement*. Alexandria, VA: Association for Supervision and Curriculum Development, 1999.

Senge, Peter M. *The Fifth Discipline: The Art and Practice of the Learning Organization*. New York: Doubleday, 1990.

Sergiovanni, Thomas J. *Moral Leadership: Getting to the Heart of School Improvement*. San Francisco: Jossey-Bass, 1992.

Sinek, Simon. *Start with Why: How Great Leaders Inspire Everyone to Take Action*. New York: Penguin, 2009.

Smalley, Gary, Norma Smalley, John Trent, and Cindy Trent. *The Treasure Tree*. Nashville: Thomas Nelson, 1992.

Smoley, Eugene R. Jr. *Effective School Boards: Strategies for Improving Board Performance*. San Francisco: Jossey-Bass, 1999.

Stoesz, Edgar. *Common Sense for Board Members: 40 Essays about Board Service*. Intercourse, PA: Good Books, 2000.
Tanner, John. *The Pitfalls of Reform: Its Incompatibility with Actual Improvement*. Lanham, MD: Rowman & Littlefield Education, 2013.
Thayer-Bacon, Barbara. *Democracies Always in the Making: Historical and Current Philosophical Issues for Education*. Lanham: Rowman & Littlefield Education, 2013.
Thomas, Kenneth W., and Ralph Kilmann. "An Overview of the Thomas-Kilmann Conflict Mode Instrument (TKI)" Available at http://www.kilmanndiagnostics.com/overview-thomas-kilmann-conflict-mode-instrument-tki .
Thomas, Paul G. "The Swirling Meanings and Practices of Accountability in the Canadian Government," in *Professionalism and Public Service: Essays in Honour of Kenneth Kernaghan*. David Siegel and Ken Rasmussen, editors. Toronto: University of Toronto Press, 2008.
———. *Performance Measurement, Reporting, Obstacles and Accountability: Future Trends and Directions*. Canberra, Australia: ANU E Press, 2009. Available online at http://epress.anu.edu.au/anzsog/performance/html/frames.php.
Ungerleider, Charles. *Failing Our Kids: How We Are Ruining Our Public Schools*. Toronto: McClelland & Stewart, 2003.
Wilmot, William, and Joyce Hocker. *Interpersonal Conflict*. 8th Ed. New York: McGraw-Hill, 2011.

About the Author

Laura Reimer brings a balance of formal education and experience as a school board member to her extensive knowledge about school boards. She is a former elected school board member with advanced education in leadership, administration, and governance, and extensive marketplace experience in governance and policy development. More important to her school board role, Laura has been active in a number of community organizations, including her children's sports, dance, and music interests, through which she built many relationships with stakeholders important to effective school board governance.

Laura has served at many levels in three school districts, including as classroom volunteer in public and private schools, parent council member and president of a French-Immersion school, and then was elected twice to school boards with sweeping victories; first to an excellent school board, and then to one that struggled through a very difficult state-initiated amalgamation. Her governance experience includes a university board of governors.

Laura's consulting work includes public school systems, alternative schools for indigenous people, First Nations school systems, private schools, and higher education. Currently an assistant professor at the University of Winnipeg in central Canada, and certified mediator, she has also worked for Canadian Mennonite University and for the University of North Carolina Greensboro, with a special emphasis on policy development, education issues, and conflict resolution applications. Laura is available for collaboration, consultation, or speaking engagements.